The
180 Life

---

*365 Pep Talks and 12
Challenges, Life-Crafted
for Transformation*

Liz Nead

neadinspiration.com

Acknowledgements

This book is dedicated to my children who gave me the fuel to succeed when I didn't believe I deserved the opportunity.

I want to thank my husband, who thinks my best life is a foregone conclusion, his vision for me intact from the beginning, even in the darkest of circumstances. I am forever grateful to my best friend Molly who always thought writing should be my main focus, my sister-friend Maggie who allows herself inspiration from my words even though it's not her thing, and my clothing-exchange friends who never flinched when I told them I was going into the inspiration business.

To my parents who really only spoke to me in parables, Bible verses, strategies and principles, I owe a debt of thanks—I would not be who I am today without your constant and consistent investment. And, to my little sister, the first to ask me to rise above my self-sabotage, I love you. You are a great visionary for my soul.

I also want to thank some friends who helped me along the way, Sean Gardner, who retweeted my quotes from the beginning, Jeff Pulver, whose conferences allowed me to see the power of raw authenticity from the stage, author and poet Caroline Rothstein for confirming my words were anchors, Saba Tekle who took me to author status and Kathy Kidd who lovingly reassured and reinforced the purpose of this book.

I am grateful for each client I have had the privilege to coach and every audience member who allowed inspiration to lift their spirits.

I humbly offer my love and gratitude to my son, Jordan, who spent his summer painstakingly pulling every quote from eight years of unwieldy social media feeds without a hint of boredom (even though it was probably terrifyingly mind-numbing) and lovingly binding it so I could see this moment.

And finally, I want to thank my God, who created me for this reason and this moment, for forgiving all my shortcomings and lifting me up where there is always light.

Table of Contents

Prologue

Lest you think I'm in a good mood all the time...

With his book, *The Power of Positive Thinking,* Norman Vincent Peale began my love affair with quotes. One or two sentences, packed with power and inspiration, designed to turn that moment, minute, day, even life around. Additionally, I was unrelentingly mothered and fathered through 800-year-old principles and made-to-control-or-at-least-influence Bible verses until eventually my father's voice blended with my thoughts and my casual conversations were sprinkled with unsolicited bits of adages and advice.

When social media added breadth to my depth and amplified my already booming voice, I was released from inspiring one or two at a time, to reaching hundreds and thousands with encouragement. I pulled the best from the greats, Shakespeare and Solomon, Eminem and Tony Robbins. Their words were a lifeline of hope, pulling me up as the recession of 2008 threatened to drag me under indefinitely. Hoping others would be inspired to look beyond the passing moment and believe in the garden on the other side of the wall, a place abundant with seeds of purpose, and the antidote for bad fortune. Wishing I could believe and experience those words as well.

It was a bad, the day of my first quotable quote. Nothing was working on that day. My gifts went unnoticed, even rejected. No money in the bank, with no hope of more in the future. Waking up each morning, rolling over to look at my husband across a cavern of distrust and misunderstanding. Implicit judgment as far as I could see, telling me I was doing it all wrong. Where was my retirement fund? My commitment to carpooling? My perfectly manicured lawn and matching set of children and husband? Then, these words, first in my mind, flowing through the clacking of fingernails on keys, on to a screen and beyond.

"Nothing feels as good as backing your plans up with actions."

Appropriating the words from no one else. My thoughts. My emotions. My lifeline. Out loud.

The 180 journey began in that moment. I resolved to create this gift from me to you. It's the flow of transformation. As I changed directions and chose thriving over surviving, the words flowed.

My Facebook friends grew from 247, to 800, to over 4000. There is always someone else with more connections, someone more famous or powerful. I'm not so concerned with the numbers as I am with the connection. To reach into your life and hold your hand. To raise your chin and look into your eyes and offer you reassurance. Or to grip your shoulder in a moment of challenge. You can do better than this. I see you. I know you. I believe in your future.

You may read these words, and think, *she is so positive. I bet she never wakes up in a bad mood.*

I confess I am always coated with a film of eager wonder. Even as I ready myself to offer my heart to the world, I am afraid of my power. I am unsure of the future. Most of the words you will read were borne out of the heaviest of circumstances, moments that sometimes threatened to steal my will to draw another breath. I was overlooked, underestimated, sometimes undermined. When the yearning to experience my dreams humbled me, I was reduced to pleading prayers drenched in tears. A paralyzing fear gripped me, thoughts my day would never come, I had made too many mistakes, squandered my potential, arrived too late to maturity.

Sometimes I could barely load the dishwasher, great and terrible questions overcoming the simple tasks of the day. Does the world really need me? What business do I have offering encouragement when I haven't truly figured it all out? Would you notice if I was gone? Would it be better if I wasn't here? Why did I need this? Why couldn't I be satisfied with something else? An unrelenting masochist. A struggling obsessive. An undeserving misfit.

This book was conceived during my 180-degree transformation, when I chose to stop hurting myself and those around me, I claimed, instead, the power and freedom that comes from a well-lived life. I wrote these words when the power was disconnected. I wrote these words after I asked my husband to leave and then begged him to come back. I wrote these words in fearful spaces of stinginess and scarcity, when no one seemed to understand or embrace my passions. I wrote these words with a bitter taste of struggle, underneath looming shadows of my failure, when a meeting planner wished she had hired someone else, when a coaching client demanded her money back. I wrote these words when I could barely catch a breath, overcome by an uncertain future journey, flanked by overwhelm and doubt.

In those moments I prayed and inspiration flowed from my deepest faith through my fingers and onto the screen. In other moments I refused the humiliation of prayer, and the words, masked in my father's voice, arrived in the form of a pep talk anyway.

It's going to be okay.
Don't think about that.
Remember your purpose.
Focus on your vision.
Choose your thoughts.
Appoint your actions.
Feel your feelings.
Stand in your moment.

For eight years, I have posted my thoughts and you, my friends and connections and followers provided a current, propelling me down my path with your likes and shares and comments. You taught me the gift of transparency and authenticity. Your engagement matched my openness. You didn't want politically infused vitriol or a condemnation of marriage. No fluff. No fake happiness. No vanity.

You are living a unique adventure, full of celebration, quiet and challenge. There is a reason, if not a purpose, to every second of your life. Through this book, I champion you. I hold up your best self to the light, for all to see, a mirror to be the change and embrace the reason you are on this planet. In these pages you will find no judgment, only a challenge to choose a path to your purpose.

And one more thing: someone asked me to group these pep talks into themes, something I will postpone until a later date. Even so, I will leave you with "The 180-Life" lessons that moved me from

certain destruction to an existence
marked by freedom.

- Your present is a payment to the
  future.
- You must be your biggest fan and
  most passionate advocate.
- Appearing to be something is not
  as important as actually being it.
- Your true state of being will reveal
  itself over time. It's impossible to
  mask.
- Doing anything for the right
  reasons will cover a multitude of
  issues.
- You can't do it alone, nor should
  you.
- You were born for a reason—you
  words and thoughts matter.
- If you wonder why you exist,
  contribute to your community and
  you will find clarity.
- You are all the parts of your whole
  being. Nurture to all of you and
  you will go further.

- You are inspiration for success. Take responsibility for what you reflect out to the universe.
- The process is far more important than a destination or an achievement.

Bless you on your journey. Release what doesn't serve you. Believe in the most powerful version of yourself. And whatever you do, don't ever give up. Valleys are an inescapable part of the mountaintops in your life. This is your transformation. This is your 180.

Month 1 Challenge:

Wake your inner child to play.

Conjure up the image of a well-loved child. Curious fingers running over bumps and divots. Running, jumping, stumbling and falling, living in the risk of movement. Eyes crinkling and squinting in observation, quick to laugh and cry.

Be unafraid to use your body and your senses to acquire new information or enjoy the moment. Step into the flow of insatiable joy and interest.

Take your lover or friends to a trampoline gym. Dance and glide around the disco ball at the roller skating rink. Sign up for a hip hop class. Take swimming lessons. Climb a tree. Set aside a few hours to play. See it as an investment in energy and clarity for your adult life.

HUNDREDS OF RISKS,
REASONS AND EXCUSES
BLOCK THE PATH TO YOUR DREAMS.

DON'T LET THE "WHY NOT'S"
DETER YOU.

FOCUS ON SHARPENING YOUR "WHY,"
AND YOUR VISION
WILL COME INTO FOCUS.

DISTRUST
ISN'T AS STRONG A PROTECTOR
AS YOU BELIEVE.

IT DISTANCES YOU FROM OTHERS,
INJECTS NEGATIVE ENERGY
INTO RELATIONSHIPS,
AND TEACHES OTHERS
TO RESPOND IN FEAR.

DON'T LAMENT YOUR
DISAPPEARING YOUTH.

CELEBRATE THE GIFT OF
GROWING OLDER.

FEAR CANNOT LIGHT THE
WAY TO SOMETHING BETTER.

ONLY LOVE CAN LEAD YOU
TO YOUR BEST LIFE.

WHATEVER YOU ARE
EXPERIENCING,
GOOD OR BAD,
IT IS TEMPORARY.

LEARN THE LESSON.
SAVOR EACH MINUTE.
THIS MOMENT WILL PASS.

IF YOU WANT THE BEST
FROM THOSE AROUND YOU,

LISTEN TO THEM,
LEARN FROM THEM,
SERVE THEM.

NOT KNOWING
SHOULD NOT BE A REASON FOR
NOT TRYING.

JUMP INTO POSSIBILITY
READY TO LEARN AND GROW.

WHAT YOU DO WHILE YOU ARE
WAITING FOR SUCCESS
IMPACTS YOUR LIFE MORE
THAN
EXPERIENCING SUCCESS.

TRYING TO BE
PERFECT USUALLY
LEADS TO...

NOTHING.

RELATIONSHIPS ARE
THE ULTIMATE CAPITAL.

CONTINUE TO INVEST IN
OTHERS DURING LIFE'S
PEAKS AND VALLEYS.

YOU WILL SURELY NEED IT LATER.

WHEN YOU HIDE
YOUR TRUTH,

YOU ROB YOURSELF
OF YOUR BEST LIFE.

GRATITUDE
UNLOCKS THE BEST
THE WORLD HAS TO OFFER.

THANK OTHERS,
GIVE THANKS,
SHARE YOUR THANKS,
AND WITNESS ABUNDANCE.

THE ABILITY TO EXPERIENCE
YOUR VISION

IS DIRECTLY RELATED TO
YOUR WILLINGNESS
TO EMBRACE
IT'S CIRCUMSTANCES.

YOUR APPROVAL
WILL NEVER MEAN
AS MUCH TO ME
AS MY OWN.

I HAVE BEEN UNDERESTIMATED
BY A GREAT MANY PEOPLE.

WHAT I KNOW IS:
THEY CAN'T SEE MY FUTURE
ANY MORE THAN I CAN.

AND I KEEP WORKING.

DON'T LET
YESTERDAY'S PAINS
KEEP YOU FROM
TOMORROW'S
SUCCESS.

WORK HARD,
BELIEVE IN RESULTS UNSEEN,
BE WILLING TO EXPLAIN
YOUR PASSION,
AND SUCCESS IS YOURS!

WHAT YOU ARE
WILLING TO DO
WILL DEFINE YOUR LIFE
MORE THAN
WHAT YOU CANNOT DO.

DISCOMFORT IS YOUR
GREATEST TEACHER.

IF YOU INVEST IN ONE THING TODAY,
LET IT BE YOU.

PRAY.
MEDITATE.
LOVE.
LEARN.

YOU WILL HAVE MORE
TO INVEST
IN THOSE AROUND YOU.

STOP ASKING PERMISSION
FROM YOUR

FAMILY,
FRIENDS AND
COWORKERS

TO LIVE YOUR BEST LIFE.

YOU HOLD THE KEY
TO YOUR DREAMS.

WHEN LIFE GETS
TOUGH,

ALIGN YOUR ACTIONS
WITH WHERE YOU ARE
GOING

NOT WHERE YOU ARE.

SOMETIMES YOU DON'T GET WHAT
YOU WANT SO YOU CAN RECEIVE
WHAT YOU NEED.

SURRENDER.
RELEASE.
ACCEPT.
RECEIVE.

EVERY MOMENT HAS A PURPOSE.

YOU CAN NEVER RETURN
TO A MOMENT IN THE PAST,
TO RELIVE EVEN ONE MINUTE.

YOU CAN FULLY EMBRACE
THE JOURNEY IN FRONT OF YOU.
TO DO BETTER,
LIVE WISER,
BE STRONGER.

FOCUS ON
PASSION-DRIVEN
EXCELLENCE
AND SUCCESS WILL
FOLLOW.

DON'T CREATE
"CONDITIONS" FOR HAPPINESS.

THE WEIGHT ON THE SCALE,
THE MONEY IN THE BANK,
A PERSON TO LOVE,
ALL GOOD.

BUT DON'T LET ANYTHING STAND
BETWEEN YOU AND
THE JOY OF THIS MOMENT.

WHEN YOU FEEL UNSURE
ABOUT YOUR NEXT STEP,

FOCUS ON HELPING OTHERS
AND YOUR FEARS WILL
MELT AWAY.

DON'T TREAT YOUR NOW
WITH DISREGARD
AND EXPECT A FUTURE
FILLED WITH WORTH.

SUCCESS IS ABOUT RIDING
THE WAVE OF POSSIBILITY,
NOT CONTROLLING
THE OCEAN OF OUTCOMES.

TRANSFORMATION OCCURS
DURING THE PURSUIT
OF YOUR DREAMS,
NOT IN THE
ACHIEVEMENT.

TURN YOUR DREAMS INTO
VISIONS,
VISIONS INTO GOALS,
GOALS INTO ACTIVITIES.

LIFE IS A SERIES OF
MOMENTS.

MAKE THIS MOMENT COUNT.

Month 2 Challenge

Invest in your future with your imagination.

Imagine having all the financial resources you need. I get it—today, your bank balance may not allow you to move forward, but nothing is stopping you from exercising your imagination and backing your vision up with research.

Turn your wish list into a price list. Think about the equipment, coaching or technology you need for your life or business. Investigate what it would take to buy a new guitar, or get new flooring in your home. Answer questions like, *how much would it cost to lease that space* or *how much would it set me back to create an adventure on the other side of the world.* Each answer, every detail, brings a bit more clarity to your beautiful visions.

IF YOU ARE IN THE BUSINESS OF
HELPING OTHERS,
HELP OTHERS FOR HELPING SAKE.

NOTHING ELSE IS SUSTAINABLE.

DON'T COMPETE WITH OTHERS.

FOCUS ON THE BEST POSSIBLE
EXPRESSION OF YOUR
POTENTIAL

AND YOU WILL ALWAYS THRIVE.

LET EVERY NO YOU HEAR FLOW
THROUGH YOU IN GRATITUDE.

THERE IS
A PERFECT YES
TO TAKE IT'S PLACE.

LONG TERM SUCCESS
OF ANY KIND
REQUIRES A WILLINGNESS
TO PURSUE EXCELLENCE
RATHER THAN PERFECTION.

YOUR LIFE WILL CHANGE WHEN
YOU REALIZE YOUR CHALLENGE
ISN'T IN A LACK OF
OPPORTUNITY,
BUT AN ABUNDANCE
OF BLESSINGS BEYOND YOUR
COMPREHENSION.

WHAT WILL YOU DO NEXT?

THE HARD TRUTH
IS ALWAYS BETTER THAN
AN EASY LIE.

DO THE RIGHT THING NOW
AND THE BEST THING
HAPPENS LATER.

FACING TODAY'S CHALLENGE
CREATES FREEDOM FOR TOMORROW.

VALUE THE OPPORTUNITIES
TO GROW AND LEARN
MORE THAN THE FINISH LINE,

AND YOU WILL NEVER
RUN OUT OF HOPE.

IF YOU ARE NOT
GENUINELY THANKFUL
FOR THE SUCCESSES OF OTHERS,

YOU MIGHT HAVE AN
ABUNDANCE PROBLEM.

THERE IS PLENTY OF
SUCCESS FOR ALL.

LIVING OUT YOUR PURPOSE
AND FAITH ELEVATES EVEN
YOUR WORST MOMENTS.

IT LIFTS YOU
OUT OF THE MUD
AND BRINGS MEANING
TO THE NOW.

YOUR JOB ISN'T TO
BECOME SOMEONE
OTHER THAN YOU ARE.

YOUR JOB IS
TO BECOME THE BEST
EXPRESSION OF YOU.

SUCCESS ISN'T
MOMENTARY.

IT'S AN ACHIEVEMENT
OF A LIFETIME.

THE BEST WAY
TO CHANGE THE MOMENT
IS TO OWN THE MOMENT.

EVERY SECOND MATTERS.
NOT JUST THE GOOD ONES.

YOUR PASSION FOR DOING
GOOD SHOULDN'T CHANGE
WITH THE NUMBER OF PEOPLE
YOU SERVE.

ALL IN.
ALL THE TIME.

YOUR DREAM IS NOT A FAR OFF
VISION.

IT'S A LIGHT AT YOUR FEET,
ILLUMINATING YOUR JOURNEY,
STEP BY STEP.

PURPOSE,
NOT PERFECTION
WILL MAKE YOU
INFINITELY MORE USEFUL
TO YOUR COMMUNITY.

YOU CAN'T CHOOSE
THE WEATHER,
THE MOODS OF OTHERS,
OR THE TRAFFIC.

YOU CAN CHOOSE
HOW YOU THINK ABOUT IT.
CHANGE YOUR DAY.
LIVE IN GRATITUDE.

GIVE YOURSELF
THE GIFT OF AUTHENTICITY.

DON'T HIDE YOUR ISSUES FROM
OTHERS OR
PRETEND THEY DON'T EXIST.

BRING THEM IN ALIGNMENT
WITH YOURSELF.

THE WORDS,

"WHAT IF"

SHOULD CREATE A SPACE OF

EXCITEMENT AND CREATIVITY,

RATHER THAN FEAR.

PEOPLE BELIEVE YOUR
ACTIONS
BEFORE THEY TRUST YOUR
WORDS.

PERSUASION BEGINS
WITH ACTION,
NOT ARGUMENTS.

WHEN YOU WITNESS A MOMENT
IN SOMEONE'S LIFE,
REMEMBER IT IS ONLY ONE STEP
IN THEIR LIFE.

YOU DON'T KNOW HOW LONG
THEY HAVE BEEN RUNNING
OR HOW FAR THEY HAVE TO GO.

WITHHOLDING LOVE
WILL CAUSE YOU PAIN.

LOVE WITH ABANDON TODAY!

FEAR CAN KEEP YOU
FROM LOOKING STUPID.

IT CAN ALSO KEEP YOU
FROM LOOKING GOOD.

POWERFUL VISION
DOESN'T COME FROM
TRYING TO PROVE YOURSELF.

TRANSFORMATIONAL,
LIFE-CHANGING VISION,
COMES FROM
BELIEVING YOUR WORTH.

SOME OF THE
BEST EXPERIENCES HAPPEN WHEN
YOU GO OFF TRACK.

BE WILLING TO EXPLORE
A FEW SHINY OBJECTS
HERE AND THERE.

YOU NEVER KNOW
WHAT YOU MIGHT FIND.

YOU MAY BE GETTING MESSAGES
THAT YOU ARE NOT
WHAT YOU SHOULD BE.

KNOW YOUR BLUEPRINT IS PERFECT.

BECOME MORE OF WHO YOU ARE, NOT
LESS.

DON'T LET
SOMEONE'S LIMITED VISION
OF YOU

DISTRACT YOU
FROM BELIEVING AND ACTING
ON YOUR BEAUTIFUL VISION
OF THE FUTURE.

LOVE DOESN'T REQUIRE
AGREEMENT OR IMITATION.

LOVE IS GOING THE EXTRA MILE
NO MATTER WHAT.

DON'T BE AFRAID TO ASK
FOR WHAT YOU WANT.

HUMANS ARE TERRIBLE
MIND READERS.

Month 3 Challenge:

Intentionally inspire others.

Whether you are struggling with change or living on top of the world, your energy is contagious. Humans are the only living beings with the gift of imagination, the ability to experience ideas. We are living reflections of the possibilities for those around us. Get intentional about your inspiration.

Make a list of the witnesses in your life, people you could inspire— colleagues, family, friends, neighbors and workout buddies. Next, make a list of purpose-driven words and activities to inspire them. Consistent workouts, healthy meals, notes of encouragement, acts of generosity. Now move into action! As you hold a light for others, you move closer to your best life.

WHEN YOU
UNDERSTAND AND ACCEPT
THE BEHAVIOR OF OTHERS
IS NOT DRIVEN BY YOU,
RATHER SHAPED BY
THEIR OWN PERSPECTIVES,
FREEDOM AND INFLUENCE
CAN BEGIN IN YOU.

MANAGING THE UNIVERSE
WILL LEAVE YOU FEELING
OVERWHELMED AND AFRAID.

FOCUS ON THE TASKS OF THE
MOMENT AND LET YOUR
VISION FIRE YOU UP!

WHEN YOU LIVE
A GENEROUS LIFE,
OFFERING THE WORLD
THE BEST OF YOUR
RESOURCES AND TALENTS,

YOUR WELL WILL NEVER
RUN DRY.

LET NOTHING
SEPARATE YOU
FROM THIS MOMENT.

ENJOY THE MINUTES
YOU ARE GRANTED.

TIME HOLDS NO
GUARANTEES.

DON'T LET
WHAT YOU THINK
OTHERS ARE THINKING

CHANGE THE GOOD
YOU ARE DOING.

WHEN YOU WORRY
ABOUT PLEASING EVERYONE,
YOU END UP
PLEASING NO ONE.

YOU HAVE THE POWER TO
CHOOSE YOUR THOUGHTS.

CHOOSE THE MOST
PRODUCTIVE AND
POSITIVE THOUGHTS
YOU CAN,
AND WATCH YOUR REALITY
CHANGE FOR THE BETTER.

HARMONY ISN'T FOUND
IN AGREEMENT.

HARMONY FLOWS
WHEN YOU ALLOW OTHERS
THE OWNERSHIP OF THEIR
OWN PERSPECTIVES.

REMARKABLE SUCCESS
GROWS

FROM THE SEEDS OF
DAILY, CONSISTENT
ACTIONS.

LIFE IS NOT RACE
AGAINST OTHER
HUMAN BEINGS.

LIFE IS AN
OPPORTUNITY
TO SERVE OTHERS
WITH YOUR PURPOSE.

WHETHER YOU DO WHAT YOU
WERE MEANT TO DO,

OR YOU MOVE BEYOND WHAT
YOU WERE NOT MEANT TO DO,

BOTH ARE A GIFT.

DON'T SIT ON THE
SIDELINES
AND PICK APART
THE EFFORTS OF OTHERS.

SAVE YOUR ENERGY AND
ATTENTION
TO RELEASE SOMETHING
FANTASTIC INTO THIS
WORLD.

I AM NOT ALWAYS IN A GOOD MOOD.
I DON'T ALWAYS SEE THE DREAM JUST
AROUND THE CORNER.
MY HOUSE IS NOT ALWAYS CLEAN.
I DON'T ALWAYS LOVE MY BODY.
I FORGET SOMETHING EVERY DAY.
I SOMETIMES EAT WHEN I'M NOT
HUNGRY.

BUT, BEING PERFECT IS BORING,
DON'T YOU THINK?

DO YOU WANT TO LIVE A
RADICAL LIFE?

REPLACE ARGUING WITH LOVE.

REPLACE MANIPULATION
WITH UNDERSTANDING.

REPLACE EXCLUSION
WITH ACCEPTANCE.

ACCEPT EVERYTHING YOU ARE,
AND EVERYTHING YOU HAVE
EXPERIENCED,
HAS A PURPOSE BOTH FOR TODAY
AND THE FUTURE.

ACCEPT THE DIVINE
RESPONSIBILITY AND POWER
FOR THIS MOMENT.

SILENCE DOESN'T EQUAL
"NO."

SOMETHING IS HAPPENING,
YOU JUST CAN'T SEE IT.

BE READY FOR ACTION.
DON'T GIVE UP AND
KEEP FOLLOWING UP.

EMBRACE YOUR AGE
BY EATING WELL,
WORKING OUT,
LOVING YOUR LOVES,
ENJOYING YOUR CHILDREN,
LIVING OUT YOUR PURPOSE,
CONNECTING WITH FRIENDS
AND OFFERING GRATITUDE
FOR ALL YOU HAVE.

DON'T ASSUME
THE ROLE OF DYSFUNCTION
SO SOMEONE ELSE CAN FEEL
LIKE A BETTER PARENT,
SIBLING, COLLEAGUE OR
FRIEND.

YOUR BEST LIFE INSPIRES.

WHEN YOU ALLOW PEOPLE TO
LOVE YOU,
INVEST IN YOU,
CHALLENGE YOU,

YOUR LIFE WILL BE RICHER
AND YOU WILL BE STRONGER.

EMPOWERMENT FLOWS
FROM STANDING
ON THE FOUNDATION
OF YOUR PURPOSE
AND LIFTING OTHERS UP.

I'D RATHER BE STRONG THAN
SKINNY.

I'D RATHER BE TRUSTED THAN
ADMIRED.

I WILL CHOOSE IMPROVEMENT
OVER COMFORT.

HERE'S TO THE PURPOSE IN YOUR
LIFE.

DON'T BE AFRAID
OF LIVING YOUR DREAM.

BRINGING YOUR "DOER"
AND YOUR "BELIEVER"
TOGETHER IN HARMONY
CREATES MAGIC.

YOU WILL BE REMEMBERED
BY THE SPEED OF YOUR SMILE,
YOUR WILLINGNESS TO HELP,
YOUR ABILITY TO UNDERSTAND.

IF YOU WANT TO BE MORE
CONSISTENT,
YOU BEGIN BY BEING MORE
CONSISTENT.

MAKE IT EASY
FOR GOOD THINGS
TO COME INTO YOUR LIFE.

LEAVE THE SKEPTICISM
AND DOUBT
FOR OTHERS.

INSTEAD,
HEAD UP THE WELCOMING
COMMITTEE FOR
ALL THINGS FABULOUS.

REAL BEAUTY
RADIATES FROM
A SENSE OF PURPOSE,
A COMPASSIONATE SPIRIT,
SPIRIT-FILLED EYES,
A BELLY FULL OF HUMOR,
AND A BODY THAT WALKED
THIS EARTH WITH BRAVERY.

IF YOU SAY NOTHING ELSE,

SAY THANK YOU.

IT MAKES ALL THE
DIFFERENCE SOMETIMES.

LET OTHERS
BE SAFE
IN THEIR ROUTINE.

TAKE COMFORT IN YOUR
PURPOSE-DRIVEN
ADVENTURES.

YOU DON'T
DEMAND RESPECT,
YOU COMMAND RESPECT.

TREAT EVERYONE
AS IF THEIR
WILDEST DREAMS
MAY COME TRUE.

JUST BECAUSE
YOU HAVEN'T DONE IT BEFORE,
OR WITNESSED IT YET,

DOESN'T MEAN
IT'S IMPOSSIBLE.

Month 4 Challenge:

Invest in yourself spiritually.

Too often, we associate our spiritual life with the doorway of the nearest place of worship. And while I personally enjoy Sundays with my church community, our inner life requires a richer and deeper investment. Continuing to crank your life-machine without spiritual investments anchors a burnout in your future.

Create a spiritual investment plan. Set up a place for reflection or meditation. Select a few books focused on personal development or gratitude. Buy a beautiful journal. Find a Bible study or book club. Write out a prayer list of gratitude and requests. Carve out time each day to journey inward and take care of your mind and heart. Wild and urgent productivity will give way to focus, purpose and balance.

SUCCESS

IS WHAT HAPPENS

WHEN YOU ARE BUSY

GIVING YOUR BEST

RIGHT NOW.

YOU DON'T NEED
TO EARN THE RIGHT
TO START OVER.
YOU JUST DO IT!

DON'T WAIT FOR SOMEONE
IMPORTANT OR FAMOUS
TO VALIDATE YOUR DESIRE
TO DO SOMETHING GOOD
IN THE WORLD.

THE THOUGHT
IS VALIDATION ENOUGH.
ACT ON IT.

SOMETIMES,
ALL YOU NEED TO KNOW
IS YOU WILL NOT
BE GIVING UP TODAY.

IF YOU DON'T HAVE A GOAL,
YOUR FEAR
WILL CREATE ONE FOR YOU.

HAPPINESS FOR OTHERS
IS A PATHWAY FOR
SUCCESS,
ABUNDANCE.
AND JOY
IN YOUR OWN LIFE.

THE GREATEST JOY IN LIFE
IS LOOKING FORWARD
TO DOING
SOMETHING GOOD,
NOT RECEIVING
SOMETHING GOOD.

IF YOU DO THINGS
FOR THE RIGHT REASONS,
YOU WILL RARELY REGRET
WHAT YOU HAVE DONE.

ENJOY WHAT YOU HAVE
AND YOU WILL RECEIVE
MORE OF WHAT YOU ENJOY.

STRESS AND PAIN SURROUND US.
SHINE YOUR LIGHT TODAY.

BE LOVING,
EXPANSIVE,
AND HOPEFUL.

YOUR COMMUNITY NEEDS YOU!

IF YOU ARE WAITING
FOR CIRCUMSTANCES TO
BE PERFECT
BEFORE YOU GET STARTED,

YOU AREN'T GOING TO
GET MUCH DONE
IN THIS LIFETIME.

WHEN YOU DO THE THINGS
THAT SCARE YOU,
OTHER THINGS
WILL SCARE YOU LESS.

PREPARE FOR YOUR DREAMS
WITH CONSISTENT ACTIONS
AND YOU WILL BE READY
FOR ALL YOUR DREAMS
TO COME TRUE.

OBLIGATION
IS THE DUTY AND PRIVILEGE
OF RELATIONSHIPS.

PROGRESS HAPPENS
IN INCHES,
NOT MILES.

YOUR BEST LIFE STARTS
IN THIS MOMENT.

I'D RATHER SPEND
TIME WORKING OUT,
THAN GETTING MY NAILS DONE.

#INVESTMENTS

TRY NOT TO SACRIFICE
PEOPLE
FOR SCHEDULES AND LISTS.
IT WON'T PAY OFF
IN THE LONG RUN.

IT'S NEVER TOO LATE
TO LIVE YOUR PURPOSE.

YOU HAVE
AN ORIGINAL ENERGY
EXPERIENCED BY THE WORLD
AROUND YOU.

STEP INTO THAT ENERGY
WITH LIGHT AND LOVE
TODAY.

WHEN YOU SEE A NEED,
YOU MAY WANT TO HELP WITH
ACTION OR TRUTHS.

DON'T FORGET TO LISTEN.

IT MAY BE YOUR MOST
POWERFUL TOOL
FOR CONNECTION AND
INFLUENCE.

BE IN THE MOMENT TODAY.
DON'T LOOK FORWARD TO ANOTHER
MOMENT.
JUST EXPERIENCE THIS PRESENT
AS A GIFT.

YOU ARE YOUNGER
THAN YOU WILL EVER BE
IN THE FUTURE.
YOU KNOW MORE
THAN YOU HAVE EVER KNOWN.
MOVE FORWARD IN THAT POWER.

IT BECOMES MORE LIKELY
YOU WILL LOVE
WHAT YOU HOLD PRECIOUS
WHEN YOU LIVE IN THE FEAR
YOU WILL LOSE IT.

THERE IS MORE THAN ENOUGH
OF EVERYTHING YOU NEED.

YOU WILL NEVER HAVE
ALL THE ANSWERS.
PLAN FOR SUCCESS
AND GET IN THE GAME!
THE ANSWERS YOU SEEK
WILL BE REVEALED
THROUGH ACTION.

GET OFF THE SIDELINES AND
JUMP IN TODAY!

DON'T WAIT FOR
THE PERFECT MOMENT.
YOU ARE PERFECT
FOR THIS MOMENT
IN YOUR LIFE.

LOOK FOR INSPIRATION TODAY.

SEEK IT OUT.

DON'T WAIT FOR IT
TO COME TO YOU.

SOCIAL MEDIA OFFERS YOU
THE PRIVILEGE TO INFLUENCE OTHERS IN
A POSITIVE WAY!

THINK ABOUT THE RIPPLES YOU CREATE
WITH YOUR WORDS AND IMAGES,
THE NUMBER OF PEOPLE
WHO WILL BE TOUCHED
BY YOUR THOUGHTS
AND HEALTHY ENERGY.

IF YOU HAVE A LESSON TO LEARN,
IT WILL CONTINUE TO SHOW UP
THOUGH PEOPLE
AND CIRCUMSTANCES
UNTIL YOU FIGURE IT OUT.

BETTER TO LEARN THE LESSON THAN
TO RATIONALIZE
THE MOMENT.

WHEN SOMETHING SCARES YOU,
DON'T AVOID IT.

THE HARD TRUTH
IS ALWAYS BETTER
THAN THE WORRY
IN YOUR HEAD.

IT'S TIME WAKE UP
AND START LIVING!

FACE RISKS,
TAKE STEPS IN FAITH,
STEP INTO YOUR TALENT
WITH FEARLESS EFFORT,
AND ACT AS IF YOU
BELIEVE AND HOPE
FOR THE BEST.

IF YOU WANT THE BEST OUT OF
THE PEOPLE AROUND YOU,

LISTEN TO THEM,
SERVE THEM,
LEARN MORE FROM THEM.

THEY HAVE SO MUCH TO OFFER,
THEY ONLY NEED TO KNOW
YOU ARE WILLING
TO NEED THEM
AND ACCEPT THEIR HELP.

Month 5 Challenge:

Make space for your best life.

Accumulation is a natural outgrowth of abundance. Your space is likely packed with things no longer serving you. I imagine there is only so much space in life and when you clutter it up with holey socks and old makeup, there is no room for what you really want. Why find the best thing when the good-enough is sitting in it's place?

De-clutter your life. Expired spices and sauces. Old blushes, mascara tubes and eye shadows. Sweaters and jeans you hope to fit in someday. Linens and bedding that no longer fit your bed or style. Discard, donate or repurpose your underused items. Open the door to what you want by passing on what you no longer need.

JUST BECAUSE YOU HAVE
LEARNED OR MASTERED
A LIFE-LESSON,
DOESN'T MEAN OTHERS
HAVE AS WELL.

WE ARE ALL LIVING
LIFE'S JOURNEY
AT OUR OWN PACE.

I RECOGNIZE AND EMBRACE JOY
BECAUSE I WANT YOU
TO FEEL IT WITH ME.

IT'S NOT DEPENDENT
ON THE CIRCUMSTANCES-
THAT WARM AND LOVELY
FEELING STARTING IN YOUR TOES
AND ENDS IN INFINITY.

WHEN A GROUP
BECOMES MORE IMPORTANT
THAN THE CAUSE,
IT IS THE
BEGINNING OF THE END.

RELATIONSHIPS
SHOULD NOT BE DEFINED BY
ONE OR TWO MOMENTS.

YOUR CONNECTION WITH
ANOTHER HUMAN IS
A SET OF MOMENTS,
A MIX OF UNCERTAINTY,
JOY, SADNESS, EXCITEMENT
AND SO MUCH MORE.

IF ONE PERSON BETRAYS YOU,
TAKE SOME TIME TO WORK IT OUT.

IF SEVERAL PEOPLE HURT YOU,
YOU MAY NEED TO FORGIVE THEM
AND CREATE BOUNDARIES.

IF EVERYONE IS OUT TO GET YOU,
TAKE A LOOK IN THE MIRROR.

I BELIEVE WE WERE NOT
GIVEN WEALTH
TO RETIRE EARLY
AND TAKE CARE OF OUR OWN.

USE THE AMAZING ABUNDANCE YOU
EXPERIENCE EVERY DAY
IN HEALTH, WEALTH AND FREEDOM
TO HELP AND ENCOURAGE OTHERS.

SOMETIMES YOU HAVE TO
NEED SOMEONE
TO TRULY UNDERSTAND
HOW MUCH THEY LOVE YOU.

I'D RATHER BE TIRED
FROM WORKING HARD
AND SERVING OTHERS
THAN ANYTHING ELSE.

YOUR PRESENT
IS A RESULT OF A SERIES
OF CHOICES AND MOMENTS
FROM THE PAST.

IF YOU WANT TO CHANGE
YOUR TOMORROW,
START WORKING WITH
YOUR NOW.

YOU HAVE LIMITED TIME
AND ENERGY TODAY.

INVEST IT IN ACTIONS
THAT YIELD POSITIVE
THOUGHTS,
RELATIONSHIPS AND
RESULTS.

BIG THINKERS,
BIG DREAMERS
AND BIG LOVERS MAKE FOR BIG
TARGETS.

STEP INTO YOUR GREATNESS TODAY
AND TELL THE WORLD TO FIRE AWAY!

THE FIRST STEP IN SUCCESS
IS SHOWING UP.

BE THERE,
BE PRESENT,
WITHOUT EXCUSES
OR BACKDOORS.

WHEN YOU STEP INTO Y
OUR SUCCESS-FILLED PRESENT,
EVERYTHING YOU NEED WILL ALREADY BE THERE,
WAITING FOR YOU.

IF YOU WANT TO TRANSFORM
YOUR LIFE,
YOU MUST EMBRACE REALITY
AND THEN CHANGE IT.
WISHING FOR A CHANGE,
CHANGES NOTHING.

WHEN YOU FINALLY REALIZE
YOU ARE ONLY GIVEN THIS LIFE
TO ACHIEVE YOUR PURPOSES
AND PASSIONS,
YOUR DAYS WILL TRANSFORM
INTO SOMETHING
TRULY AMAZING.

I KNOW YOU DON'T WANT
TO DO SOMETHING.

IT'S DARK EARLY TONIGHT
AND NO ONE IS GOING TO
NOTICE OR CARE
IF YOU WAIT ANOTHER DAY.

BUT YOU KNOW.
AND YOU KNOW WHY.
SO GO DO IT.
IT WILL FEEL BETTER.

FEAR IS IN YOUR HEAD.

DISAPPOINTMENT IS IN YOUR HEAD.

LOVE AND EXCITEMENT

ARE IN YOUR HEAD.

IT'S UP TO YOU TO TAKE

WHAT IS YOUR HEAD

AND TURN INTO REALITY THROUGH ACTION.

WHAT REALITY WILL YOU CHOOSE TODAY?

DON'T ALWAYS PURSUE
MORE, FASTER, BIGGER, BETTER.

THE SWEETEST INSPIRATION
IS ABOUT
CLARITY AND ALIGNMENT,
DOING THE THING
WITH THE LEAST UNKINDNESS
AND HIGHEST LEVEL OF PURPOSE.

YOU CAN BE ABSOLUTELY CORRECT
BUT WITHOUT GRATITUDE
AND APPRECIATION,
YOU WILL BYPASS
THE ENERGY OF THE MOMENT.

TODAY, PURSUE JOY
RATHER THAN PLEASURE.
CONNECT YOUR ACTIONS
TO YOUR PURPOSE
AND ALLOW GRATITUDE
TO FLOW THROUGH YOU.

ACCESS ABUNDANCE THROUGH
AUTHENTICITY.

YOU CAN'T DRAW IN
SUSTAINABLE RICHES
WITH IMPERSONATIONS.

SOMETIMES THINGS SLOW DOWN SO
OTHERS CAN STEP IN
AND BE YOUR HERO.

YOU DON'T GET WHAT YOU WANT
SO YOU WILL RECEIVE
WHAT YOU NEED.

YOU MISS THE MARK
SO YOU WILL CONTINUE DOWN THE
ROAD TO WHAT YOU DESERVE.

SURRENDER,
RELEASE,
ACCEPT,
AND RECEIVE.

IT'S ALL HAPPENING FOR A REASON.

RATHER THAN SEARCHING FOR SUCCESS,
LOOK FOR PLACES TO USE YOUR GIFTS,
TO ENCOURAGE OTHERS,
TO HELP THEM OFFER THE BEST OF
WHO THEY ARE TO THE WORLD.

DON'T WORRY ABOUT WHETHER YOU ARE
NOTICED, UNDERSTOOD, OR EVEN VALUED.

JUST KEEP OFFERING WHAT YOU HAVE
FOR THE BETTERMENT OF THOSE AROUND YOU.

SUCCESS WILL FIND YOU.

I WISH I COULD SHOW YOU HOW MANY TIMES
SOMEONE HAS INTENTIONALLY OR ACCIDENTALLY
DISREGARDED ME, MINIMIZED ME, OR
DISCOURAGED ME AT LOW MOMENTS IN MY
SPEAKING AND COACHING CAREER.

NOT PLAYING IT SAFE AND PURSUING YOUR
PURPOSE CAN BE SCARY TO OTHERS. WALKING YOUR
PURPOSE WITHOUT KNOWING ALL THE ANSWERS
CAN BE UNSETTLING TO WATCH.

DON'T GIVE UP. KEEP IT MOVING. DON'T STOP
LEARNING AND GROWING. EXPERIENCE LIFE WITH
ALL IT'S EDGES AND CONTOURS.. IT'S BETTER TO
CRY REAL TEARS THAN FAKE A SMILE. I'M PROUD
OF YOU ALREADY.

THE BEST KIND OF PEACE
DOESN'T HAPPEN WHEN EVERYTHING IS
LINED UP IN PERFECTION.

THE BEST KIND OF PEACE IS THE CALM YOU
FEEL WHEN LIFE ISN'T EXACTLY RIGHT,
WHEN FAITH IS NEEDED TO TAKE THE NEXT
STEPS.

THAT KIND OF PEACE IS TRULY A GIFT.

YOU WILL NEVER FULLY MASTER
THE HUMAN STRUGGLE-
JEALOUSY, WORRY, UNKINDNESS.

LIVE WITH HUMILITY INSTEAD.
WE ARE ALL CAPABLE OF
THE BEST AND WORST
OF THE HUMAN EXPERIENCE.

YOU WILL NEVER GET IT RIGHT ALL
THE TIME.
YOU WILL NEVER IT ALL RIGHT THE
FIRST TIME.

YOU CAN MAKE ANY
EFFORT OR CIRCUMSTANCE
EXACTLY AS IT SHOULD BE
WITH YOUR WILLINGNESS TO
TRY, STUMBLE, ACCEPT, ADMIT
AND GETTING UP AGAIN.

THE GOOD YOU SEE AROUND YOU
IS PROOF
OF WHAT YOU CAN
ACHIEVE AND RECEIVE,
NOT A SIGN THERE IS
LESS FORTUNE FOR YOU.

CELEBRATE WITH YOUR FRIENDS
AND CONTINUE TO
OFFER AND RECEIVE.

IN YOUR EFFORT TO BE
ELOQUENT AND ADMIRABLE,
DON'T FORGET TO BE REAL.

PEOPLE NEED TO SEE YOU
ATTEMPT AND FAIL,
TO STAND WITHOUT EXPLANATION,
TO HOLD YOUR PRESENT-SELF,
UNASHAMED.

KNOW THE DIFFERENCE BETWEEN
SOMETHING INCOMPREHENSIBLE
AND INCONCEIVABLE
AND SOMETHING THAT LOOKS
IMPOSSIBLE.

THE FIRST WILL
LEAD YOU TO LEARN.
THE LATTER WILL
LEAD YOU TO GIVE UP.

Month 6 Challenge:

Ask for what you need.

Reaching for what you need is not a sign of dissatisfaction. Leaning on fellow humans to achieve your dreams is rooted in strength. While it may seem easier to retreat within and depend solely on yourself, that same protection also restricts you from growth.

You were meant to thrive in community! Boldly and courageously and ask for what you need. Offer your business services and products to new acquaintances and friends. Ask for help getting your kids to their activities. Enlist a talented friend for advice or help with a home improvement project. Be direct—don't hint around— and be a specific as possible. Expect to be surprised and delighted as you open your heart to the gifts in your village and feel your strength grow with each request.

THE PROCESS OF
AUTHENTICITY AND HONOR
IN OUR RELATIONSHIP
TO OURSELVES
IS OF THE UTMOST
IMPORTANCE.

ASSUME AND EXPECT
TWO THINGS IN YOUR LIFE.

YOU WILL NEVER HAVE ALL
THE ANSWERS,
AND IT WILL RARELY GO AS
YOU PICTURE IT.

LEARN TO WORK IN
UNCERTAINTY
WITH FLUIDITY AND GRACE.

ONE HALLMARK OF A
SUCCESSFUL LIFE
IS TRYING TO DO
THE RIGHT THING
REGARDLESS OF THE CIRCUMSTANCES.

IT'S THE BEST WAY
TO STAY ON TRACK
OR GET BACK ON TRACK.

PURSUE OPPORTUNITIES
AS IF THEY ALREADY BELONG TO YOU,
BUT LET GO OF THE OUTCOME.

THE ULTIMATE RESULT
WILL PROBABLY BE BETTER
THAN YOU ENVISIONED.

EVERYTHING YOU DO MATTERS.

YOU DON'T HAVE TO YELL TO HURT SOMEONE.
YOU DON'T HAVE TO PUNCH SOMEONE TO
FOSTER THE HURT INSIDE OF THEM.

BE AWARE OF THE POWER YOU HAVE IN
YOUR COMMUNITY
AND BE RESPONSIBLE
WITH THE INFLUENCE YOU HAVE
ON THOSE AROUND YOU.

PERFECTION IS IMPOSSIBLE.

RATHER THAN TRYING TO APPEAR AS IF
YOU KNOW ALL THE ANSWERS,
AS IF YOU HAVE IT HANDLED,
CHALLENGE YOURSELF TO
LEARN THE LESSONS IN THIS MOMENT,
AND WORK ON
THE FOUNDATIONS OF YOUR LIFE.

WHEN YOU SEE SOMEONE BRIGHT AND
INSPIRING, DON'T EXPECT THEM TO BE
YOUR FIRE.
IT WILL ONLY LEAD TO
WORSHIP,
DISAPPOINTMENT,
AND INSECURITY.

INSTEAD, ASK THEM OR ALLOW THEM TO
BE YOUR SPARK
AND SHINE YOUR OWN
BEAUTIFUL LIGHT!

EXCELLENCE
MIXED WITH PURPOSE
IS THE GOAL TODAY!

TODAY LET
"GOOD ENOUGH"
NOT
BE GOOD ENOUGH.

URGENCY DOESN'T HELP YOU
GET IT DONE.
IT ACTUALLY CREATES
CONFUSION AND STRESS
AND MAKES YOU FEEL
YOU HAVE LESS TIME.

A MEASURED AND FOCUSED STATE OF MIND
WILL MAKE TIME EXPAND.
YOU CAN ONLY DO ONE THING AT A TIME.
CHOOSE IT,
FOCUS ON IT,
COMPLETE IT,
AND MOVE ON!

I DON'T RUN FOR
THE SIZE OF MY WAIST
OR THE TIME IN THE RACE,
BUT TO PUMP AIR INTO MY LUNGS
AND BLOOD THROUGH MY VEINS.

I DON'T STAND ON STAGE
FOR ATTENTION AND LAUGHS
BUT FOR THE OPPORTUNITY
TO INSPIRE YOU TO LIVE
BIGGER AND BETTER.

I DON'T LOVE FOR LOVE TO BE RETURNED
BUT FOR THE PRIVILEGE OF EXPRESSING LOVE
WHILE YOU ARE STILL HERE.

I DON'T PRAY FOR THINGS AND CIRCUMSTANCES
TO COME INTO MY LIFE
BUT INSTEAD FOR THE HONOR
TO CONNECT WITH THE PURPOSE I'M ON THE PLANET.

SET GOALS YOU AREN'T SURE OF, GOALS
THAT MAKE YOUR STOMACH TURN
AND YOUR SOUL DOUBT.
THIS IS WHERE THE GROWTH HAPPENS.

SUCCESS DOESN'T PUNCH A CLOCK
BETWEEN 9 AND 5.

IT DOESN'T CARE
HOW OLD YOU ARE OR
HOW GUILTY YOU FEEL.
IT DOESN'T CARE
HOW MUCH YOU KNOW OR
HOW MANY TIMES YOU HAVE TRIED BEFORE.

SUCCESS IS ABOUT SHOWING UP
WITH A FULL HEART,
READY TO DO WHAT IT TAKES
RIGHT NOW.

WHEN YOUR PRIORITIES
ARE OUT OF BALANCE,
EVERYTHING FEELS HEAVY.

WHEN YOU ARE ALIGNED
WITH YOUR PURPOSE,
NOTHING SEEMS IMPOSSIBLE.

DON'T LET FEAR
KEEP YOU FROM LOOKING AT
YOUR BIG PICTURE.
IT'S ALWAYS BETTER
TO UNDERSTAND REALITY,
THAN TO IGNORE
THE STUFF THAT SCARES YOU.

TRUTH IS ALWAYS POWER.

SO MUCH OF
RELATIONSHIP STRESS
COMES FROM THE ASSUMPTION YOU
HAVE TO BE
ALIKE IN SOME WAY.

IT WAS DIVINELY PLANNED
WE WERE ALL BORN WITH A FREE WILL
AND UNIQUE IDENTITY.
AGREEMENT SHOULD HAPPEN
NATURALLY.
ENJOY THE DIVERSITY!

JUMP INTO THE POOL OF
"WHAT IF,"
INSTEAD OF THE
"WHAT MIGHT HAVE BEEN."

IT'S OKAY TO
WONDER AND EXPLORE
LIFE BEYOND YOUR EXPERIENCE
RIGHT NOW.
LIFE IS AN ADVENTURE!

EVERYONE HAS SAID,
"NEVER AGAIN."

PROCEED WITH NEW RESPECT
FOR THOSE LIFE LESSONS
BUT DON'T CREATE BOUNDARIES
THAT PREVENT NEW
OPPORTUNITIES FOR SUCCESS.

WHEN YOU FEEL COMPELLED TO
HIDE YOUR TRUTH,
YOU ROB YOURSELF OF YOUR BEST.

YOU HAVE THE POWER
TO SEE YOUR LIFE
AS AN AMAZING GIFT OR
YOUR WORST NIGHTMARE.

WHATEVER YOU SEE
WILL BE YOUR EXPERIENCE.

YOUR LIFE IS DEFINED
MORE BY WHAT YOU DO
WITH THE DARK DAYS
RATHER THAN THE SUNNY ONES.

THERE IS SOMETHING MAGICAL
ABOUT GIVING YOUR VERY BEST
TO SOMEONE BEYOND
FINANCIAL AND
INTERPERSONAL REWARD.

CHOOSE TO USE THE POWER OF LOVE.

IT CUTS THROUGH
DISBELIEF AND APATHY.
IT'S BIGGER THAN
SKIN COLOR, CULTURE,
LANGUAGE AND STATUS.

LOVE DRIVES US TO REACH OUT,
LIVE BIG, JUMP BEYOND.

ROOTING FOR SOMEONE
DOESN'T REQUIRE YOU
TO OPENLY AND BLINDLY
SUPPORT EVERYTHING THEY DO.

SOMETIMES YOU MIGHT HAVE TO SAY,
"YOU ARE BETTER THAN THIS."

WHEN YOU THINK IN ABUNDANCE,
YOU KNOW THERE ARE
LIMITLESS POSSIBILITIES
AND OTHERS' SUCCESS
IS A VISION OF
WHAT IS POSSIBLE.

AS YOU NEAR
THE ACHIEVEMENT OF YOUR DREAMS, YOU
WILL EXPERIENCE
A SLIVER OF FEAR
THAT COMES WITH
DARING TO WANT MORE.

IT'S NORMAL!

DON'T LET THAT FEAR
KEEP YOU FROM EXPERIENCING
YOUR LIFE'S BEST JOURNEY.

DON'T PLACE ALL OF YOUR
WORTH
INTO ONE ASPECT OF YOUR LIFE.

YOUR BEST LIFE IS FILLED WITH
A DIVERSITY OF EXPERIENCE.

IF YOU STAND FOR ANYTHING, CLAIM
THREE THINGS:
GRACE,
SAFETY
AND COMPASSION.

FOR JUST WHEN YOU THINK YOUR
INTELLECTUAL AND SPIRITUAL POSITION
IS UNWAVERING,
SOMETHING WILL HAPPEN TO YOU
THAT WILL PUSH YOU TO NEED
GRACE, SAFETY AND COMPASSION
FROM OTHERS.

YOUR SUCCESS IN LIFE WILL DEPEND
ON THREE THINGS:

WHAT YOU ARE WILLING TO DO.
WHAT YOU ARE WILLING TO AVOID.
WHAT YOU ARE WILLING TO
ENVISION.

DREAMS ARE A WHISPERING,
A CALLING TO THE YOUR PURPOSE.

IT'S A SACRED LIGHT
ILLUMINATING THIS MOMENT.
JUST TAKE ONE STEP ON THE JOURNEY.
THE DREAM WILL CONTINUE TO
LIGHT YOUR WAY.

FINISH WHAT YOU START.

NOT TO AVOID JUDGEMENT
OR PROVE ANYTHING.

FINISH FOR THE FEELING OF
SELF-LOVE KNOWING
YOU GAVE IT ALL YOU GOT.

FROM THERE,
YOU CAN LOVE THE WORLD.

Month 7 Challenge:

Take a laugh break.

Stand in front of the mirror and smile. A few seconds will pass before a feeling bubbles up to match your grin, reach your eyes and pour back into your heart. You will find it is almost impossible to feel a certain odd flavored joy from what started as a contrived smile.

Laughter is a necessary exercise for your spirit. Don't restrict your smile as you see your child do something endearing. Enjoy a comedy on television or at the theater. Recall silly moments with a dear friend over a glass of wine and allow the giggles to spill over between you. Play an incorrigible game with your family and tease one another mercilessly. Fly above the daily rigors of life and infuse the moment with the delicious energy in laughter.

A POSITIVE PERSON
DOESN'T IGNORE THE PROBLEM, ALWAYS
READY WITH A CHEERY COMMENT
AND A HAPPY SMILE.

POSITIVE PEOPLE
FACE EVERY SITUATION WITH A BELIEF
THERE IS ALWAYS A BEST WAY,
A REASON FOR LIFE,
A PURPOSE TO CIRCUMSTANCES
AND IT'S THEIR JOB TO FIGURE IT OUT.

DON'T DERIVE YOUR INTELLECTUAL
AND EMOTIONAL SAFETY
FROM KNOWING ALL THE ANSWERS.

THE ART OF LIVING
IS IN THE QUESTIONS!

CHANGES BEGIN IN YOUR HEART,
TAKES HOLD IN YOUR MIND,
AND DEVELOPS ROOTS
DURING ACTION.

DON'T PRAY FOR ABUNDANCE.
DON'T PRAY FOR MORE.

ASK THAT YOU WILL SEE
THE BLESSINGS ALREADY
SURROUNDING YOU.

USE COMPARISON
AS A POINT OF
INSPIRATION,
NOT IRRITATION.

INAUTHENTICITY IS A WAY
TO DISOWN YOURSELF.
YOU ARE SAYING,
"I AM NOT GOOD ENOUGH.
I AM EMBARRASSED OF WHO I AM."

YOU ARE NOT A MISTAKE.
YOU ARE DIVINELY INSPIRED.
WHATEVER YOU WANT TO COVER UP
WITH FEIGNED IMPERFECTION
IS EXACTLY WHAT SOMEONE
NEEDS TO SEE AND HEAR,
RIGHT NOW.

I USED TO BE A CHRONIC AVOIDER,
HOPING WHATEVER I WAS FACING
WOULD MAGICALLY GET EASIER.

IT NEVER DID.

FEEL GRATITUDE FOR THE FREEDOM
THAT COMES WITH THE TRUTH.
DO THE RIGHT THING NOW,
AND THE BEST THING HAPPENS LATER.

THE KEY TO SUCCESSFUL,
LONG TERM RELATIONSHIPS
ISN'T HARMONY,
IT'S BALANCE.

MAKE SPACE FOR DISAGREEMENT,
EVEN FIGHTING, PASSION,
LAUGHTER AND AGREEMENT.

STRIVE TO KNOW EACH OTHER,
NOT GET ALONG WITH EACH OTHER
AND YOUR RELATIONSHIPS WILL GROW.

WITHHOLDING FORGIVENESS
AND HOLDING JUDGEMENT
ONLY POISONS YOU.

FORGIVE,
EVEN IF IT IS SILENTLY.
RELEASE AND RENEW.
YOU WILL FEEL BETTER
IMMEDIATELY.

RELEASING EXPECTATIONS OF
OTHERS WILL CHANGE YOUR LIFE.

IT WILL LEAVE YOU WITH
EXTRA ENERGY TO CREATE HEALTHY
EXPECTATIONS OF YOURSELF.

SUCCESS STARTS WITH YOU.

BEING GOOD AT A SPORT DOESN'T MEAN YOU HAVE STRONG
CHARACTER.

BEING REALLY SMART DOESN'T MEAN YOU KNOW HOW TO
HONOR YOUR RELATIONSHIPS.

BEING GOOD-LOOKING DOESN'T MEAN YOU HAVE A
CONSCIENCE.

HAVING A LOT OF MONEY DOESN'T MEAN YOU KNOW HOW
TO GIVE WHOLEHEARTEDLY.

ACHIEVING AN AWARD DOESN'T INCREASE YOUR WORTH.

STOP ELEVATING PEOPLE TO GOD-LIKE STATUS. NO MATTER
WHAT THE CIRCUMSTANCES, THEY ARE JUST HUMAN.

INSTEAD, FOCUS ON BEING THE BEST HUMAN YOU CAN BE.

TRANSFORMATION IS NOT
A DESTINATION.

IT IS HAPPENING WITH
EVERY STEP OF YOUR
JOURNEY.

DISCOURAGEMENT GROWS
FROM A LACK OF OPPORTUNITIES.

IF YOU WANT TO INFUSE YOUR DAY
WITH OPTIMISM FOR THE FUTURE,
WORK ON INCREASING YOUR
OPPORTUNITIES BY CONSISTENTLY,
PERSISTENTLY AND UNAPOLOGETICALLY
OFFERING YOUR TALENTS
WHEREVER AND WHENEVER NEEDED.

THE BEST PART OF THE SUCCESS JOURNEY IS NOT IN THE
ACHIEVEMENT.

IT'S THE PERMISSION TO HOPE DURING A DIFFICULT
SITUATION.
IT'S THE EXCITEMENT AS YOU REALIZE YOUR DREAM IS
ACTUALLY POSSIBLE.
IT'S THE FEELING OF SATISFACTION YOU FEEL WHEN YOU
REACH A MILESTONE.
IT'S THE CELEBRATION AS YOU CROSS THE FINISH LINE WITH
THOSE YOU LOVE.
AND, IT'S THE STRENGTH AND CONFIDENCE AS YOU SET NEW
DREAMS IN PLACE.

THE JOURNEY IS REALLY MORE DELICIOUS THAN THE
ACCOMPLISHMENT.
TAKE A MOMENT FOR THANKS IN THIS MOMENT AS YOU
PURSUE YOUR DREAM.

YOU HAVE THE FREEDOM TO
CHANGE YOUR CIRCUMSTANCES.

YOU DECIDE HOW YOU WANT TO FEEL
ABOUT THE VALUE OF YOUR PERSON
AND YOUR LIFE.

CHANGE MAY NOT BE EASY
AND IT MAY NOT BE FAIR.

BUT CHANGE IS ALWAYS POSSIBLE.

YOUR BEAUTY LIES IN
WHAT MAKES YOU UNIQUE.

DON'T SUCCUMB TO
CONFORMITY
OR HIDE YOUR LIGHT.

POWERFUL VISION
DOESN'T COME
FROM TRYING TO
PROVE YOURSELF WORTHY.

POWERFUL,
LIFE-CHANGING VISION
COMES FROM
BELIEVING IN YOUR
IMMEASURABLE WORTH.

GOOD ADVICE DOESN'T ALWAYS
COME IN A SHINY PACKAGE,
EASY TO RECEIVE.

DON'T LOSE THE OPPORTUNITY
TO LEARN AND IMPROVE
BECAUSE YOU DON'T LIKE
THE WAY IT'S DELIVERED.
KEEP GROWING
AND KEEP MOVING!

I AM ALWAYS
ENCOURAGED AND ENERGIZED
BY THOSE WHO BELIEVE IN
ME.

STAND IN SUPPORT
FOR THOSE YOU LOVE.
IT WILL MAKE
ALL THE DIFFERENCE.

DON'T CREATE ENEMIES BECAUSE
YOU HAVE BECOME
COMFORTABLE WITH THE FIGHT.

THERE SHOULD ALWAYS BE
TIME AND SPACE
FOR PEACE IN YOUR LIFE.

IF YOU CAN,
BE GRATEFUL TO BE
LIVING IN
THE IMPROVED AFTER PICTURE.

AND KNOW YOUR TODAY WILL
SOON BE A BEFORE PICTURE
AND THERE WILL BE ANOTHER AFTER,
EVEN MORE BEAUTIFUL.

AS YOU CONSIDER A CHANGE,
REMEMBER YOU ARE TAKING A
RISK ON YOURSELF,
NOT YOUR CIRCUMSTANCES.

YOU ARE YOUR GREATEST ASSET.

WHEN SOMEONE ASKS FOR YOUR HELP,
CONSIDER IT A PRIVILEGE.

IT MEANS THEY HAVE OPENED UP
THEIR LIFE AND
LET YOU SEE THEIR NEED.

BE HONORED AND TAKE ACTION.

BE THANKFUL FOR THOSE
RELATIONSHIPS
GIVING YOU THE FREEDOM
TO BE COMPLETELY AUTHENTIC.

TRY TO OFFER THAT SAME
FREEDOM AND SPACE
TO JUST BE THEMSELVES
AROUND YOU.

IT'S A GIFT!

DREAM BIG, AS BIG AS YOU CAN.

FOR ONCE YOU REALIZE YOUR DREAM,
YOU WILL SEE
IT WAS NOT AS WILD
AS IT SEEMED
AND YOUR NEXT VISION
WILL BE EVEN MORE EXPANSIVE.

SOMETIMES YOUR CIRCUMSTANCES
CAN SEEM LIKE
ONE CRAZY AND CONFUSING CIRCUS.

DON'T GET DISTRACTED
BY THE SIDESHOWS!

KEEP YOUR EYE ON
WHAT IS IMPORTANT TO YOU.

LEADERS ARE OFTEN
MISUNDERSTOOD OR
MISCHARACTERIZED.

IT COMES WITH
STEPPING OUT IN VISION.

JUST KEEP SERVING OTHERS
AND IT WILL WORK ITSELF OUT.

DON'T BE SO HARD ON PEOPLE
WHEN THEY MAKE MISTAKES
AND YOU WON'T BE AS AFRAID
TO MAKE ONE YOURSELF.

SOMETIMES WE LOOK AT
SOMETHING OUTSIDE OURSELVES
WHEN GOD JUST WANTS US TO
BELIEVE IN OURSELVES.

WHEN SOMEONE WANTS TO
WORK HARD
AND REACH FOR THE STARS,
LET THEM.

DON'T TRY TO PULL THEM
BACK IN THE NAME OF
REALISM.

YOU HAVE NOTHING TO LOSE
AND EVERYTHING TO GAIN.

THE HONOR OF INFLUENCING OTHERS
BEGINS WITH UNDERSTANDING
AND RESPECTING THE VIEWPOINTS
AND POSITIONS OF OTHERS.

LIFE IS COMPLEX BUT IT DOESN'T
HAVE TO BE COMPLICATED.

WHEN YOU EXPECT THINGS TO BE
CONFUSING AND HARD,
THEY WILL BE.

EXPECT YOU WILL HAVE THE
TIME, ENERGY, AND SPACE
FOR WHAT IS IMPORTANT TO YOU.

Month 8 Challenge:

Plan to give back.

Acts of service are often a casualty of a busy schedule. Without a plan, we spend our free moments relaxing until the roller coaster begins again and we miss the chance to contribute our resources and gifts. No matter what your circumstance, someone in your community needs you right now.

Open your eyes to the needs around you. Make a list of places you can volunteer during a free afternoon. Carry a small bag of toiletries and a few dollars to give to someone in need. Keep a box by the door for unneeded clothes. Invite your lover or friends to work at a food pantry before you enjoy a date or ladies night. Giving back is way to feed your soul, bringing you perspective and connection.

TRYING TO LOOK PERFECT
ONLY DISTANCES YOU FROM
THE PERFECTION YOU DESIRE.

DON'T HIDE YOUR JOURNEY.

CAPITALIZE WHAT MAKES YOU DIFFERENT,
STRIVE TO LEARN EVERYTHING YOU CAN
AND DO YOUR BEST IN THIS LIFE.

THAT, MY FRIEND,
IS PERFECTION.

REAL LIFE DOESN'T HAPPEN IN
STATUS UPDATES
AND PHOTO UPLOADS.

IT'S A MINUTE-BY-MINUTE EFFORT.

CONTINUE TO PURSUE EXCELLENCE,
EMBRACE PROGRESS,
AND STRIVE TO DO BETTER
THAN YOU DID YESTERDAY.

TAKE RESPONSIBILITY ONLY
FOR YOUR OWN ACTIONS
AND RELEASE OTHERS
TO DO THE SAME.

ABUNDANCE DOESN'T COME
BY HOARDING WHAT YOU HAVE.

GIVE IT ALL
AND YOU WILL GET IT ALL BACK
AND MORE!

YOUR DAILY EXPERIENCE
IS A RESULT OF YOUR
CONSISTENT BEHAVIORS.

WHAT DOES YOUR REALITY
TELL YOU ABOUT
YOUR INVESTMENTS?

YOU STAND ALONE AS YOU.

YOU AREN'T YOUR WORK,
YOUR FAMILY OR YOUR LOCATION.

THEY CAN REFLECT YOU
BUT THEY DON'T DEFINE YOU.

SINCE YOU CAN'T SEE THE FUTURE,
WHY NOT DO YOUR BEST
RIGHT NOW?

DON'T EVER BE AFRAID
TO IMAGINE
THE BEST POSSIBLE SCENARIO
FOR YOU.

WHEN YOU ARE FEELING DOWN,
DON'T RESIST YOUR EMOTIONS.

THE PROCESS OF PRETENDING YOU AREN'T
MAD OR SAD WILL ONLY EXHAUST YOU.

JUST FEEL WHAT YOU FEEL,
KNOWING IT WILL PASS,
TRUSTING IN THE PURPOSE
OF THE MOMENT.

PERCEIVED EFFORT
AND HOW YOU FEEL ABOUT IT,
IS USUALLY WHAT MAKES
TASKS DIFFICULT.

STOP THINKING,
JUMP IN AND
GET IT DONE!

DON'T CONFUSE
GRATITUDE WITH OPTIMISM.

GRATITUDE IS AN
ACKNOWLEDGEMENT FOR
WHAT YOU LOVE AND BENEFIT
FROM IN YOUR LIFE.

WHAT ARE YOU THANKFUL FOR
TODAY?

CHANGE AND SELF-
IMPROVEMENT
WILL HAPPEN WHEN YOU
MAKE SPACE IN YOUR
PRIORITIES,
NOT YOUR SCHEDULE.

LEARNING IS LIFE,
YOUR OXYGEN,
YOUR REASON TO LIVE.

EVEN IF YOU ARE NOT INTENTIONAL
IN YOUR GROWTH,
YOU ARE STILL LEARNING.
WHY NOT DIRECT, CHOOSE YOUR LESSONS?

SEEK OUT EXPERTS, READ VORACIOUSLY, ASK
UNAPOLOGETICALLY.

RAISE YOUR HAND AND
CLAIM YOUR GOD-GIVEN RIGHT TO LEARN.

RESOLVE TO ACCEPT YOURSELF
WHOLLY AND COMPLETELY.

ACCEPT ALL THAT YOU ARE, ROUGH
EDGES, IMPERFECTIONS,
UNSIGHTLY BLEMISHES IN YOUR
PERSON AND YOUR SOUL.

YOU CAN'T GET THE BEST OF YOU
WITHOUT EMBRACING THE WHOLE
OF YOU.

BE VIGILANT IN YOUR THOUGHTS.
DON'T ALLOW A STREAM OF NEGATIVE
CHATTER BECOME A FLOOD OF STRESS.

PREPARE A SET OF THOUGHTS,
KEEP YOUR MIND ON GRATITUDE,
VISIONS OF THE FUTURE,
PROOF OF THE POSITIVE.

STOP THINKING YOUR EXPRESSION
OF PAIN AND CONCERN,
IS BETTER THAN BEING JUDGED.

THE VALLEY IS PART OF
THE MOUNTAIN.

RIGHT NOW,
THERE IS A LESSON
YOU SHOULD BE LEARNING.

EVERY MOMENT IS TEACHING YOU
SOMETHING ABOUT WHAT WORKS AND
WHAT DOESN'T.
IT WILL CONTINUE TO SHOW UP,
A LITTLE LOUDER EACH TIME.

WHAT WILL YOU LEARN TODAY?

IF YOU WANT TO CHANGE YOUR LIFE,
CHOOSE A PATH
AND STICK WITH THE PLAN.

CHANGING YOUR ENTIRE LIFE IN
TWO DAYS SOUNDS TEMPTING
BUT YOU WILL HAVE TO ACT AND
BEHAVE WITH CONSISTENCY
BEFORE YOU WILL SEE THE RESULTS.

DON'T LOOK FOR OUTSIDE APPROVAL.

SEEK INNER PRIDE.
DO THE RIGHT THING.
SPEAK UP WHEN NEEDED.
LEARN TO LISTEN.
FOCUS ON YOUR VISION.
BE BOLD WITH YOUR PURPOSE.
LIVE IN HUMILITY AND GRATITUDE.

YOUR PATH WILL OPEN UP BEFORE YOU AND
YOU WILL BE ABLE TO SEE FOR MILES.

DON'T SILENCE YOUR VOICE
OUT OF ANTICIPATION
SOMEONE MIGHT DISAGREE.

THE WORLD IS INCOMPLETE WITHOUT
YOUR VOICE IN THE
CONVERSATION.

WHEN YOU LOOK AT MY LIFE,
I WANT YOU TO SEE TWO THINGS:

FIRST, I BOLDLY PUT OUT MY BEST
EFFORT WITHOUT REGARD FOR
ACHIEVEMENT OR FAILURE.

SECOND, I AM HERE TO SUPPORT YOU
IN YOUR SUCCESS OR DEFEAT.

ANXIETY AND FEAR
MAY DRIVE YOU TO WANT
TO BE ORDINARY.

REMEMBER,
THE OPPORTUNITY
TO BE GREAT
IS NOW.

IF YOU WANT TO IMPROVE,
SURROUND YOURSELF WITH PEOPLE WHO
STIMULATE YOUR VISION AND
CHALLENGE YOU TO TAKE BIGGER LEAPS
THAN YOU ARE COMFORTABLE WITH.

YOU MIGHT FEEL BIGGER AROUND
PEOPLE WHO ARE SMALLER,
BUT YOU AREN'T GROWING.

I DON'T BELIEVE IN THE OLD
ADAGE, "FAKE IT TILL YOU MAKE IT."

I WILL FULLY EMBRACE
WORKING AND LIVING,
AS IF THE BEST OUTCOME IS POSSIBLE.

STAND A LITTLE STRAIGHTER, BE
UNAFRAID OF WHAT YOU NEED TO LEARN,
LIVE BOLDLY,
AND LIVE WITH INTEGRITY.

LIFE IS A PRIVILEGE,
NOT A REASON TO COMPLAIN.

WHAT ARE YOU GOING TO DO
WITH THOSE SECONDS, MINUTES,
HOURS AND DAYS?

ENJOY IT,
USE IT,
SACRIFICE IT
AND LEAVE A LEGACY.

DON'T KEEP YOUR DREAMS IN A BOX, DEFINED BY
THE KNOWLEDGE
YOU HAVE TODAY.

FOLLOW UP WHEN SOMEONE REACHES OUT TO YOU.
ACCEPT SUCCESS FROM UNEXPECTED PLACES.
BE WILLING TO EXPLORE PATHS OF UNCERTAINTY.
REACH OUT AND ASK FOR HELP AND ADVICE.
BET ON YOUR DRIVE AND TALENT, NOT YOUR
ABILITY TO PREDICT THE FUTURE.

YOUR DREAM SHOULDN'T BE MANAGED, IT SHOULD
BE HONORED.

WHENEVER POSSIBLE,
PUT THE CARE FOR OTHERS
BEFORE THE NEED
TO EXPRESS YOUR OPINION.

YOU CAN'T LIVE FOR THE PEOPLE IN
YOUR LIFE,
CHILDREN,
PARTNERS,
FRIENDS.

YOU CAN LIVE TO SERVE THOSE
AROUND YOU WITH YOUR GIFTS.
DEVELOP THOSE STRENGTHS AND
THOSE YOU LOVE
WILL BENEFIT FROM THE LEGACY.

ANYTHING IN YOUR DREAMS WILL BE

A COMBINATION OF

HARD WORK,

BARRIERS,

PERSISTENCE

AND COURAGE.

WHILE YOU CAN'T KNOW
WHAT THIS DAY WILL HOLD,
YOU CAN BE READY.
TO LEARN,
LOVE,
WIN,
LOSE,
LIVE.
EMBRACE IT ALL IN
GRATITUDE AND ABUNDANCE
WILL FILL YOUR EVERY CORNER.

DON'T EVER BE AFRAID TO TRY.

THE RESULTS, WHETHER GOOD OR BAD,
WILL ONLY LEAD
TO ANOTHER OPPORTUNITY.

TRADE PERFECTION FOR
RELEVANCE AND
USEFULNESS.

"NOT" BELIEVING IN YOURSELF IS
REALLY A BELIEF IN NEGATIVE VIEW
OF YOURSELF AND THE POSSIBILITIES.

TAKE CHARGE OF YOUR BELIEFS.
LEAN IN TO STRENGTH,
PERSEVERANCE, AUTHENTICITY,
TRUTH, BRAVERY AND PURPOSE.

THINK OF SOMETHING GOOD IN
YOUR LIFE AND SMILE.

YOU CAN'T ALWAYS BE HAPPY
BUT YOU CAN
CHOOSE JOY RIGHT NOW.

A LIFE UNEXAMINED IS A WASTE.

LOOK FOR MEANING, LESSONS AND
OPPORTUNITIES FOR IMPROVEMENT.

DON'T FORGET TO NOTICE AND
CELEBRATE YOUR OWN
PERSONAL DEVELOPMENT.

GIVING THANKS IN DARK MOMENTS
WILL CREATE INDESCRIBABLE POWER.

WHEN YOU FEEL LIKE GIVING UP,
TAKE A MOMENT AND BREATHE IN
EVERYTHING RIGHT IN YOUR LIFE.

IT IS GIVING UP AND
TAKING CONTROL
AT IT'S BEST.

GRATITUDE UNLOCKS THE WORLD.

WHEN YOU THANK OTHERS,
WHEN YOU ARE TRULY THANKFUL FOR
THE OPPORTUNITY TO MOVE FORWARD,
WHEN YOU ACKNOWLEDGE THE UPSIDE
IN A DARK SITUATION,
WHEN YOU INFLUENCE OTHERS TO SEE
THE GOOD AROUND THEM,
YOU WILL SEE WHAT ABUNDANCE
REALLY IS.

DON'T TRY TO LIVE A RISK-
FREE LIFE.

WHILE YOU ARE PROTECTING
YOURSELF FROM PAIN,
YOU ARE ALSO LOSING
OPPORTUNITIES.

IN ORDER TO GRASP YOUR VISION, YOU
MUST DO TWO THINGS:

DECLARE AND ASK.

DECLARE WHAT YOU WANT
SPECIFICALLY AND OFTEN.
ASK OTHERS TO HELP YOU
ALONG YOUR JOURNEY.

DON'T LEAVE YOUR DREAMS UNSPOKEN.

WHEN SOMETHING UNEXPECTED
POPS UP,
DON'T ASSUME IT IS BAD.

MANY GOOD EXPERIENCES
ARE A RESULT OF
MANY UNFORESEEN
CIRCUMSTANCES.

DON'T GET OVERWHELMED BY THE
MAGNITUDE OF
YOUR RESPONSIBILITIES
OR YOUR DREAMS.

LET EXCELLENCE LEAD YOU,
FOCUS ON ONE THING AT A TIME
AND DO IT WELL.

Month 9 Challenge:

Seek feedback.

Sometimes we learn to shield ourselves from our unmistakable truth because we don't want to see the impact of our personality or we are simply afraid of our greatness. Perhaps some well meaning advice cut too closely to your tender heart. It's easy to hide from the valuable perspectives of others, but it could be keeping you from more fulfilling journey.

Ask a prolific friend to review your manuscript. Create a few questions and send them out to trusted colleagues. Go to an expert and find out whether you have what it takes to be a chef or an artist. Dig through what you receive and choose to take on what will make you better and move you towards your dreams. There are mirrors all around you. Gather the courage to see yourself as you really are.

JUST AS CIRCUMSTANCES
CAN CHANGE YOU,
YOU CAN CHANGE YOUR
CIRCUMSTANCES.

LIVE OUT YOUR DREAMS
FEROCIOUSLY.

ANYONE CAN ACHEIVE SUCCESS
AND AMASS FORTUNES.

NOT EVERYONE CAN
MAINTAIN THEIR INTEGRITY,
ORIGINALITY AND
SENSE OF SELF.

NOW THAT'S IMPRESSIVE.

MOST ANXIETY COMES FROM
IMAGINING AND RECOUNTING
SCENARIOS WE HAVE NO CONTROL
OVER.

FOCUS ON WHAT YOU CAN
SUSTAIN AND BUILD
IN THIS MOMENT.

THE MOST DIRECT ROUTE TO EXCELLENCE
IS BY TACKLING THE TASKS YOU DON'T
FEEL LIKE DOING WITH
INTENTION,
ATTENTION,
AND INTEGRITY.

MISUNDERSTANDING,
DISCOURAGEMENT,
AND UNCERTAINTY
WILL NOT CHANGE YOUR PURPOSE.

DO YOUR BEST IN THIS MOMENT,
AND YOU WILL EXPERIENCE
WHAT IS BEST FOR YOU.

PERSONAL AND PROFESSIONAL
BRANDING IS AS MUCH
RECEIVING A "NO"
FROM ONE GROUP
AS IT IS RECEIVING
ACCEPTANCE FROM ANOTHER.

YOU CANNOT EFFECTIVELY BE
ALL THINGS FOR ALL PEOPLE.

ENCOURAGEMENT IS NOT BEST EXPRESSED
IN GRAND GESTURES.

SUPPORT ONE ANOTHER SMALL,
INTENTIONAL, AND PERSONAL
CONNECTIONS.

ANYONE CAN BEGIN AN
AMAZING JOURNEY.

CHECK BACK
A FEW MONTHS OR YEARS LATER
AND THE JOURNEY HAS BECOME
ORDINARY
BUT THE TRAVELERS WHO REMAIN
ARE TRULY EXTRAORDINARY.

YOU WILL NEVER BE ABLE TO DETERMINE
THE WORTH OF A PERSON
BY THE CUT OF THEIR CLOTHING
OR THE SIZE OF THEIR HOME.

THEIR SUCCESS CANNOT BE FULLY DEFINED
BY THEIR IMPRESSIVE PROFESSIONAL TITLE
OR THE EXPANSE OF THEIR REACH.

IF YOU FEEL JOY
WHEN YOU ARE IN THEIR PRESENCE,
YOU MIGHT BE ON TO SOMETHING.

DON'T STAND IN THE WAY
OF YOUR OWN HAPPINESS
BY NOT FORGIVING
SOMEONE YOU LOVE.

COMMIT TO THE ACTION
RATHER THAN THE
CIRCUMSTANCE
AND YOUR LIFE
WILL SLOWLY BUT SURELY
CHANGE FOR THE BETTER.

WHEN SOMETHING GOES WRONG,
DON'T ASK YOURSELF, "WHY ME?"

STRENGTH IS NOT BUILT
RUNNING ON A FLAT SURFACE ON A
SUNNY, WINDLESS DAY.

TRUE STRENGTH IS BUILT ON THE HILLS,
IN THE RAIN AND WIND,
WHEN YOU DON'T FEEL LIKE IT,
WHEN NO ONE UNDERSTANDS,
WHEN NO ONE BELIEVES.

STRENGTH IS BUILT DURING RESISTANCE.

SO WHEN YOU ARE HAVING ONE OF THOSE DAYS,
CONSIDER YOURSELF CHOSEN.
AND STARTING CLIMBING THE HILL.

YOUR PASSION FOR ALL-OUT,
FULL-THROTTLE, BEST-EFFORT ACTION IS
WHAT CONNECTS YOU TO SUCCESS, NOT
POSITIVE OUTCOMES.

TAKE HEART AS YOU HEAR THOSE
NO'S, MAYBE'S AND NOT NOW'S.

LISTEN TO YOUR HEART,
PROPELLING YOU FORWARD.

YOUR BEST LIFE IS ALREADY IN MOTION.

DON'T EXAGGERATE YOUR SUCCESS.
DON'T MAKE YOUR MARRIAGE LOOK HARMONIOUS. DON'T
LIE ABOUT HOW MUCH WEIGHT YOU HAVE LOST. DON'T ACT AS
IF YOUR BUSINESS IS GOING SMOOTHING THAN IT APPEARS,
BECAUSE YOU CAN'T BEAR THE THOUGHT OF BEING HONEST
WITH A COLLEAGUE.

HOW WILL YOU REACH OUT FOR HELP WHEN YOU LOOK "FINE?"

HOW MUCH ENERGY DO YOU THINK YOU SPEND ACTING
DIFFERENT THAN YOUR BEING?

THE BEST WAY TO CHANGE THE MOMENT IS TO OWN THE
MOMENT. EVERY SECOND MATTERS.
NOT JUST THE GOOD ONES.

YOU DON'T NEED TO
BE FEARLESS.
ONLY COURAGEOUS.

BE THE OPPORTUNITY FOR CHANGE
IN SOMEONE ELSE'S LIFE.

TAKE A CHANCE THEY NEED YOU
TO BE THE MOST AUTHENTIC
EXPRESSION OF YOU IN ORDER TO
BECOME THE BEST THEY CAN BE.

DON'T PICK AND CHOOSE WHOM
YOU SHOW CONSIDERATION AND RESPECT,
BASED ON THEIR USEFULNESS TO YOU.
YOU WILL CERTAINLY
MISJUDGE SOMEONE'S VALUE.

INSTEAD, TREAT EVERYONE
AS IF THEY ARE PRICELESS
AND USE YOUR TALENTS TO SERVE THEM.

THE RETURN ON YOUR
INVESTMENT IS LIMITLESS.

THE ENERGY IN
FEAR,
JOY
AND LOVE
CREATE RIPPLES FAR BEYOND
THIS PRESENT MOMENT.

WHAT ENERGY ARE YOU
INJECTING IN YOUR LIFE?

DON'T LET YOUR SENSE OF ORDER
GET IN THE WAY OF YOUR SUCCESS.

EAT BREAKFAST FOR DINNER.
WORK OUT IN THE
MIDDLE OF YOUR WORKDAY.
MAKE LOVE IN THE KITCHEN.

WHO CARES WHEN YOU DO WELL?
DO WELL WHENEVER YOU CAN.

DON'T GIVE INTO
MOMENTARY FEELINGS OF
UNEASINESS.

CLOSE YOUR EYES,
BREATHE DEEPLY,
AND RELEASE GRATITUDE
FOR EVERYTHING GOOD IN YOUR LIFE.

YOUR EXISTENCE GOES BEYOND
THE WELLBEING
OF YOU AND THOSE YOU LOVE.

DARE TO DIP INTO
THE SEA OF NEED
ON THE PLANET
AND MAKE A DIFFERENCE.

DON'T LET THE FEAR OF HEARING NO
PREVENT YOU FROM PURSUING
WHAT YOU DESIRE
OR DOING WHAT IT TAKES.

YOU CAN'T PREDICT
WHAT WILL HAPPEN NEXT
BUT YOU CAN PLAN TO DO WELL
AND DO RIGHT IN THIS MOMENT.

OPEN YOUR MIND AND HEART
TO THE REASON YOU ARE HERE.
BE READY TO GIVE AND RECEIVE.

YOUR PURPOSE ON THE PLANET
WILL CERTAINLY SHOW UP.

IF YOU VIEW LIFE
AS A SERIES OF PEAKS,
(HOLIDAYS, MARATHONS,
WEDDING, PROMOTIONS),
YOU MIGHT GET ADDICTED TO THE
"HIGH" OF THE NEXT BIG EVENT.

EACH STEP IN LIFE HAS EQUAL VALUE.
SUBMERGE YOURSELF
IN THE PURPOSE OF THIS MOMENT.

AN OFTEN OVERLOOKED INGREDIENT
TO SUCCESS IS FLEXIBILITY.

DO WHAT YOU NEED TO DO,
GO WHERE YOU NEED TO GO,
LEARN WHAT YOU NEED TO LEARN.

SUCCESS IS USUALLY USHERED
IN WITH A LITTLE HUSTLE.

DON'T FOCUS ON WHAT
YOU CAN'T CHANGE.

MAKE LOVING AND KIND CHOICES
WHERE YOU CAN
AND LIFE WILL SEEM SWEETER.

YOUR OWN WORDS AND ACTIONS
ARE ONLY A RESULT OF WHAT
YOU FILL YOUR MIND.

DON'T CONFINE YOUR PROGRESS
TO ONE PATH.

SUCCESS OFTEN TAKES
UNEXPECTED AND CREATIVE
FORMS.

THE LESS YOU EXPECT OF OTHERS,
THE MORE THEY WILL DELIGHT YOU.

Month 10 Challenge:

Create time for reflection.

I confess, even in my best life, I find many things I want to change. Too many cloudy days in a row and the drips of angst gather speed and begin to flow. True transformation can be choked by your wishes for an alternate reality.

Carve out an hour for reflection or save a few minutes at the end of each day this week. Create three lists—a fair acknowledgement of the circumstances you want to change, those areas you want to maintain and grow and the vision of what you want but don't have. Keep your list nearby and review it every few weeks, adding tasks to your to-do list moving you closer to what you desire. Say a prayer of thanks as you push for improvement. Root your vision for change in gratitude and you will see growth.

POWERFUL LEADERS
THRIVE ON SEEING THE PEOPLE
AROUND THEM
SOAR.

IF YOU MAKE TIME FOR WHAT
YOU SHOULD DO,

YOU WILL HAVE PLENTY OF TIME
FOR WHAT YOU WANT TO DO.

THE OPPORTUNITY TO IMPROVE
IS NOT FAILURE.

IT'S SUCCESS IN ACTION.

ENJOY THE SECOND CHANCES
YOU GET IN LIFE.

IT'S AN OPPORTUNITY TO
FEEL GRATEFUL,
DO BETTER,
LIVE WISER.

FOCUS IS ABOUT KEEP YOUR EYE ON
YOUR WHY,

WHEN YOUR
WHAT,
WHEN,
WHERE
AND WHO,

ARE CHANGING.

AS YOU CREATE SOMETHING NEW
AND BEAUTIFUL IN YOUR LIFE,
NOTICE THE MOMENTS OF
SILENCE AND EMPTINESS WHERE
YOUR OLD LIFE EXISTED.

YOU MUST LET GO OF WHAT
DOESN'T WORK
IN ORDER TO ACHIEVE
ABUNDANCE
IN YOUR BEST LIFE.

YOU WON'T FIND A SHORTCUT TO
YOUR BEST LIFE.

RELATIONSHIPS, CAREERS, HEALTH,
REPUTATIONS...

ALL RESULT FROM
INTENTIONAL
AND CONSISTENT
ACTIONS.

IF YOU HAVE DREAMS,
BIG OR SMALL,
GET USED TO BEING
UNDERESTIMATED.

YOU ARE SEEING YOUR NEW LIFE
BEFORE EVERYONE ELSE DOES.

DON'T WORRY ABOUT
GETTING IT RIGHT.

PROGRESS COMES FROM
JUMPING IN,
TRYING,
DUSTING YOURSELF OFF
AND TRYING AGAIN.

WHEN YOU CATCH A GLIMPSE OF
SOMEONE'S JOURNEY,
DON'T ASSUME
YOU KNOW THE WHOLE STORY.

THEY COULD BE IN THEIR
FIRST STEPS OF THE RACE
OR PUSHING THEMSELVES
TO THE FINISH LINE.

SEEK TO UNDERSTAND AND SUPPORT THEM
WHERE THEY ARE IN THEIR JOURNEY.

COMMITMENT IS A WORD YOU
USE TO DESCRIBE
YOUR RESPONSE
IN MOMENTS OF DIFFICULTY.

IT IF WAS EASY,
WE WOULD CALL IT VACATION.

THE WORLD AROUND CAN ONLY REFLECT

WHAT YOU THINK OF YOURSELF.

IT'S BETTER SOMEONE IS
DISAPPOINTED
IN A TRUTHFUL DESCRIPTION
OF YOUR PAST
THAN TO HAVE THEM TO
BELIEVE IN AN
EASY VERSION OF UNTRUTH.

IF YOU WANT YOUR LIFE TO CHANGE
RIGHT NOW,

FINISH WHAT YOU HAVE STARTED.

WHEN YOUR CHARACTER OR
CONTRIBUTION IS
QUESTIONED,

DON'T MOVE
TO PROVE YOURSELF.

LET YOUR LIFE
BE YOUR WITNESS.

AS YOU PURSUE YOUR VISION,
KNOWING WHY,

IS MORE IMPORTANT THAN
WHY NOT.

THE PRACTICE OF
DOING THE RIGHT THING
LEADS TO FREEDOM.

YOUR ACTIONS REVEAL
YOUR PRIORITIES,
NOT YOUR WORDS.

WHAT IS IMPORTANT TO YOU TODAY?

I'M NOT HERE TO SEEK APPROVAL.

I'M HERE TO LIVE MY PURPOSE.

DON'T LET ANYONE
CONVINCE YOU NOT TO SHINE
AT YOUR MAXIMUM BRIGHTNESS.

YOU AREN'T DOING THEM ANY FAVORS.
THEY NEED YOUR LIGHT.

DREAM OF THE FINISH
BUT FOCUS ON THIS STEP.

WHILE YOU WERE
PRETENDING TO BE PERFECT,

YOU MIGHT HAVE LOST
THE CHANCE TO
LEARN SOMETHING.

THERE IS A WEALTH OF RETURNS
FOR THOSE WHO INVEST IN OTHERS
WITH AN OPEN HEART.

DON'T LET ANYONE TELL YOU
BECAUSE YOU ONCE WERE,
YOU CAN'T BE.

NO ONE CAN
CHOOSE YOUR LIMITS
BUT YOU.

DON'T SCHEDULE
EVERY MINUTE OF YOUR DAY.

LEAVE SPACE FOR THE UNEXPECTED.

OPPORTUNITIES DROP INTO SPACE,
NOT BUSYNESS.

YOU AREN'T HERE TO WIN.
YOU ARE HERE TO CONTRIBUTE.

FAITH ISN'T SO IMPRESSIVE
WITHOUT A LITTLE DOUBT
TO KEEP HER COMPANY.

WHAT YOU FEAR,

LIVES INSIDE YOUR HEAD.

DEAL WITH IT THERE FIRST.

IF YOU DON'T NEED GRACE EVERY DAY,
YOU AREN'T RISKING ENOUGH.

DON'T THINK BECAUSE
YOU AREN'T FAMOUS,
YOU AREN'T INFLUENTIAL.

YOUR WORDS, ACTIONS, PLANS AND IDEAS
ARE NECESSARY TO
CREATE REAL CHANGE IN THIS LIFE.

DON'T WAIT FOR SOMEONE WITH
MORE MONEY OR RECOGNITION
TO SOLVE THE PROBLEMS YOU SEE.

Month 11 Challenge:

Begin the journey to overnight success.

The millionaire businessman, a best-selling author, the newly crowned athlete or actor, they leave us feeling we are standing in the wrong line for achievement. We question the universe. Why can't I experience overnight success?

Begin your own journey to overnight success. Create a list of 30 small but powerful tasks and activities to knock out over a period of several months—cleaning out a drawer, getting a work out in, sending a sexy text to the one you love or putting away five dollars. Commit to doing at least one every day. Imagine the transformation stemming from 30 or 60 purpose-driven steps.

BARRIERS AND RESISTANCE
ARE OPPORTUNITIES
DISGUISED AS PROBLEMS.

DON'T BE IMPRESSED
WITH PEOPLE WHO SEEM FAR AHEAD
OF YOU ON THE SUCCESS JOURNEY.

INSTEAD BE INSPIRED
BY THOSE YOU MEET
AND LET THOSE MOMENTS
CREATE A BRIDGE BETWEEN
YOUR DAILY EXPERIENCE
AND YOUR FUTURE SUCCESS.

STOP WAITING FOR
SOMETHING TO HAPPEN.
STEP INTO ACTION.

EVEN WHEN YOU FEEL YOUR
PROGRESS IS PAUSED
FOR A MOMENT,
THERE IS ALWAYS SOMETHING
YOU CAN DO TO PREPARE
YOURSELF FOR SUCCESS.

IF YOU CAN NOTICE AND
ENJOY THE LITTLE THINGS,
YOU WILL SURELY ENJOY
THE REST OF YOUR LIFE.

IF YOU WANT TO ENJOY YOUR
OWN SUCCESS,
START BY LETTING YOURSELF
EXPERIENCE JOY
FOR THE SUCCESSES OF OTHERS.

INSPIRATION IS BEST PASSED ON
THROUGH EXAMPLE,

NOT WORDS.

WHEN YOU SEEK TO UNDERSTAND,

YOUR NEED TO BE UNDERSTOOD
WILL RECEDE.

GRATITUDE WILL HELP YOU
HANDLE THE FUTURE,
NO MATTER WHAT THE
CIRCUMSTANCES.

LIVE A LIFE SO BEAUTIFUL,
PEOPLE ARE UPLIFTED
JUST FOR HAVING KNOWN YOU.

IF YOU ARE WAITING
FOR THE PERFECT MOMENT
TO MAKE A CHANGE IN YOUR LIFE,
YOU WILL PASS UP A GREAT MANY
OPPORTUNITIES FOR TRANSFORMATION.

THE PERFECT TIME FOR A
POSITIVE CHANGE IS NOW
AND THE PERFECTION YOU SEEK
CAN BE FOUND IN YOUR
OPEN-HEARTED AND HONEST ACTIONS.

LIVE A LIFE THAT DOESN'T MAKE
YOU WISH FOR YESTERDAY.

INVEST IN YOUR FUTURE
WITH A PURPOSE-DRIVEN
COMMITMENT
TO THIS MOMENT.

MOST OF YOUR "I CAN'TS"
COME FROM
A LACK OF INFORMATION.

LEARN AND RISK
BEFORE YOU DENY YOURSELF
THE CHANCE TO FLY.

THE MOST IMPORTANT
WORDS AND PROMISES
ARE THOSE YOU SAY
TO YOURSELF.

TRY TO DO SOMETHING PROACTIVE
FIRST THING IN YOUR DAY.

IT'S LIKE PAYING YOURSELF FIRST,
IN TIME.

IT'S OKAY TO TRY AND FAIL,
BUT IT'S A WASTE OF TIME
NOT TO TRY AT ALL.

AS YOU ARE
INTERACTING WITH
OTHERS TODAY,
DON'T HOLD BACK.

IT'S GOOD TO BE AROUND
GIGGLY, JOYFUL LOVE.

EXPERIENCE THE PRIVILEGE OF
BELIEVING IN SOMETHING
BIGGER THAN YOU.
IT DOESN'T MAKE
YOU PITIFUL OR WEAK.

IT MAKES YOU INFINITELY
POWERFUL.

IF YOU WANT TO FEEL NEEDED,
REACH OUT AND
HELP SOMEONE AROUND YOU.

THERE WILL NEVER BE
A SHORTAGE OF NEEDS,
I PROMISE YOU!

YOUR LIFE NEEDS YOUR ATTENTION!

DON'T SPEND ALL YOUR TIME
THINKING ABOUT THE NEXT MOMENT.

FOCUS ON THE LESSONS AND JOYS
OF THE NOW.

BEFORE YOU THINK ABOUT GETTING
THE ACCEPTANCE OF OTHERS,

WORK ON FULLY
ACCEPTING YOURSELF.

YOU WON'T GET ANYWHERE
PRETENDING TO BE
HAPPY,
HEALTHY,
OR FOCUSED.

CHANGE HAPPENS IN THE
BEING, NOT APPEARING.

THE RACE ISN'T WON WHEN
THINGS ARE EASY,
BUT WHEN YOU DON'T FEEL
LIKE PUSHING THROUGH,

AND DO IT ANYWAY.

LET YOUR SELF-IMPROVEMENT
GROW FROM SELF-LOVE,
RATHER THAN LOATHING.

THE ROOTS OF LOVE
YIELD BEAUTY AND
INSPIRATION.

IF YOU GET UP READY TO LEARN,
YOU WILL NEVER FEEL STUPID.

IF YOU TAKE YOUR DREAMS SERIOUSLY.

THEY WILL BECOME YOUR REALITY.

DON'T ONLY DO YOUR BEST
WHEN YOU THINK
SOMEONE IS WATCHING.

SOMEONE IS ALWAYS
WATCHING.

I WON'T PLAY SMALLER
SO YOU CAN FEEL BIGGER,
BUT I WILL PLAY BETTER,
SO YOU CAN PLAY BETTER.

IT TAKES MORE EFFORT
TO LOOK LIKE YOU KNOW
WHAT YOU ARE DOING,
THAN IT TAKES TO LEARN
WHAT YOU NEED TO BE DOING.

DO YOU KNOW HOW POWERFUL YOU ARE?
LOOK SOMEONE IN THE EYE AND OFFER
THEM A BIG, BEAUTIFUL SMILE.
REALLY LISTEN TO THEM AND ASK
QUESTIONS.

THEN, SIT BACK AND WATCH WHAT
HAPPENS.

YOU ARE MORE POWERFUL THAN YOU
THINK.

DON'T PRAY FOR THINGS.
PRAY FOR OPPORTUNITIES.

Month 12 Challenge:

Add vegetables to your diet.

Too often, food is mistakenly associated with calorie restriction when nourishment fuels our best life. Every morsel is a place of connection back to our community and planet. Each bite is an opportunity for gratitude.

Your body and brain needs the best food to function at the highest level. Veggies are the superstars of nutrition, contributing to fighting aging and disease while boosting quality of life such as better sleep and a clearer mind.

Add three or four vegetables to your diet each day. Research the benefits of your choices and personalize them to your health. Strive to create dishes that make you want to share them with others.

DON'T LET YOUR WORRIES ABOUT
WHAT MIGHT HAPPEN,
RUIN YOUR ENJOYMENT
ABOUT WHAT IS HAPPENING.

YOU NEED NOT LOOK TO THE RIGHT OR

THE LEFT TO ASSESS

HOW YOU ARE DOING.

LOOK INWARD.

THAT'S WHERE THE BLUEPRINT LIES.

I WOULD RATHER FAIL ONE
THOUSAND TIMES
AND REACH MY POTENTIAL,

THAN TO ARRIVE SAFELY
AT THE END OF MY LIFE
WITHOUT
THE MAGIC OF MY PURPOSE.

MOST OF THE TIME,
YOU WILL HAVE TO TAKE
YOURSELF SERIOUSLY
BEFORE EVERYONE ELSE WILL.

I'M NOT HERE
TO FIND ANYTHING.

I'M HERE TO OFFER
MY ENERGY,
MY PURPOSE,
MY GIFTS,
MY VISION
AND MY FOCUS.

What are you training your body to expect?

Your body has physiological responses to your thoughts- fear, happiness, anger, anxiety, gratitude, determination.

Do you tell yourself someone is out to get you, good times are bound to end, you have to stay ahead of the problems and anxiety?

Or, are you surrounded with reasons to be thankful, opportunities to connect and people who want to help?

You may not be in control of what is happening around you, but you ARE in control of how you think about it.

We tend to one of two things
with our seconds.

When things are good,
we cling to the present.
When life gets hard,
we wish for the moment to pass.

Here's what I know for sure:
No matter what, every moment moves on with the same
frequency.
Everything will pass, good or bad.

Make your seconds count:
savor the moment,
or learn from the moment.

I am not available for competition
my friends.
I will not fight over opportunities
like starved dogs over a bone.

I believe in the abundance
I see around me every day.
Your success is a vision
and gateway to my success.
My actions are for the edification
of my community.
Replace competition with expansion!

ALL the power is in the present!

You can't set your priorities
and then mechanically
make choices about the moment.

Each second is a balancing act and
you have to pay attention to the needs
of THIS moment to get the most out of
life and experience the gratitude
embedded in what you have
in front of you.

Don't create boundaries for learning.
Don't say-
I don't do that.
That's not for me.
I'm too old for that.
I just don't get it.

Dive in! Your brain THRIVES on new
information. Give it a nice big
heaping bowl of NEW STUFF every day.

You will be the coolest 90 year old on
the planet.

THERE IS AN ENERGY FLOW, A FREQUENCY,
WHERE TRUE SUCCESS LIVES.
IT CANNOT BE ACCESSED THOUGH FEAR OR
URGENCY OR A NEED FOR VALIDATION.

IF YOU WANT TO TAP INTO THAT CRAZY, EXPANSIVE,
AWE-INSPIRING STREAM OF SUCCESS,
YOU MUST FEEL GRATITUDE FOR EVERYTHING YOU HAVE.

EVERY LESSON YOU HAVE LEARNED.
EVERY PERSON YOU HAVE ENCOUNTERED.
EVERY BREATH YOU HAVE THE PRIVILEGE TO DRAW IN TO YOUR
LUNGS.

EVERY MOUNTAIN, VALLEY AND VISTA.

NOW, WHAT WILL YOU DO WITH IT?
STAKE YOUR CLAIM FOR YOUR BEST LIFE!

IT'S NOT ABOUT BEING THE BEST
THAT WILL HELP YOU
REACH YOUR SUMMIT.

IT'S ABOUT GIVING YOUR BEST,
WHATEVER THAT IS, EVERY DAY.

DON'T TEACH YOUR CHILDREN HOW TO GET ALONG
WITH OTHER BY STUFFING THEIR FEELINGS,
AVOIDING CONFLICT AND CLINGING TO LIKE-
MINDED PEOPLE.

INSTEAD, HELP THEM TO
LEARN TO CREATE EXCELLENCE THROUGH THEIR GIFTS,
SERVE OTHERS WITHOUT EXPECTATION,
EXPRESS THEIR FEELINGS,
ELEVATE THE BEHAVIOR OF THOSE AROUND THEM,
FORGIVE AND FORGET,
LOVE WITHOUT SUFFOCATION,

STAND ALONE AND KNOW THEMSELVES.

DON'T LET PEOPLE WHO JUDGE
YOU FOR YOUR TENACITY
DETER YOU FROM ACTION.

BE FEARLESS,
CREATIVE
AND PERSISTENT
AS YOU OFFER YOUR
GIFTS TO THE WORLD.

STOP LOOK FOR A SUCCESS-FAIRY,
HANDING OUT POSITIVE RESULTS.

ACTING ON YOUR DREAMS AND
VISIONS IS A PRIVILEGE ONLY
HUMANS CAN ENJOY.

TAKE ADVANTAGE OF THE
OPPORTUNITY.

WHEN THINGS ARE GOING WELL,
YOU MAY FEAR WANTING MORE,
AND DISTURBING THE BALANCE OF
YOUR PEACEFUL EXISTENCE.

DON'T LET THAT FEAR KEEP YOU
FROM CONTINUING ON TO YOUR
BEST LIFE.

THERE IS NO SHORTAGE
OF DIVISIVE TOPICS
TO TEAR US APART.

SPEND TIME
BUILDING BRIDGES
THROUGH RESPECTFUL DIALOGUE TODAY.

CONTINUOUS URGENCY
WILL EVENTUALLY KILL YOU.

ACCEPT THE UNCERTAINTY
OF THE JOURNEY
ANDDO WHAT YOU CAN
IN THIS MOMENT.

WHILE YOU ARE
WAITING FOR ANSWERS,
MAKE SURE YOU
TAKE ADVANTAGE OF
THE SOLUTIONS
ALL AROUND YOU.

YOU HAVE A GAME
YOU CAN PLAY
BETTER THAN ANYONE ELSE.

YOU WERE BORN WITH IT.

YOU'LL NEVER BE QUITE AS GOOD
PLAYING SOMEONE ELSE'S GAME.

DO YOUR THING!

DON'T CLUMP TOGETHER IN
GROUPS OF PEOPLE WHO LOOK AND
ACT LIKE YOU.

THERE IS SO MUCH YOU CAN OFFER
EACH OTHER IF YOU SIMPLY WORK
HARD ALONGSIDE EACH OTHER,
ENCOURAGING AND INSPIRING
WITH YOUR
KINDNESS AND PRESENCE.

Happy St. Patrick's Day to Nead Inspiration

One more story.

I got my first "hate mail" a few days after St. Patrick's Day, in the seventh year of Nead Inspiration. It was a perfect Midwestern spring day, the kind that makes a walk to the mailbox an enjoyable experience. I turned my head to the sun and soaked in a few momentary strands of sunlight as I shuffled in my husband's flip-flops to the end of the drive.

Eager and expectant I searched through a handful of circulars and catalogs for a thank you card or check. There, tucked between a Victoria Secret "magazine" and an invitation to the new pizza place down the street, was an ordinary white business envelope addressed to Liz Nead.

My name and address carefully scripted in black pen, I didn't notice there was no return address right away, distracted by the scattering of round and leaf-shaped green stickers. Shamrocks. A St. Patty's day surprise. Squeezing the rest of my mail under my arm, I ripped open the flap, thinking somewhat judgmentally of all the poor people who didn't see their mailbox as anything but a receptacle of purposeless mail and bills. I lived for days like this, proof of my visions so long ago.

My first hate mail came on a single plain white sheet of copy paper, minus the date, name or signature. The writer had attended a networking group I keynoted a week earlier, where I had spoken about my commitment to a purpose-driven, visionary life.

It was a triumphant experience in many ways, speaking to a small collection of women who met monthly, its name inspired by the idea all ladies are connected and equal and valued. They asked me to speak for, well nothing, not as a reflection of my value of course but more as a reflection of their available funds and I agreed, because after ten years this was thankfully no longer the norm for me and more importantly because I would be able to see five women who had been by my side in those early, lean years of my inspirational adventure.

The networking group had promoted the event well, and word spread through the city and surround suburbs, of the little luncheon held curiously in a very nice rented space at a nursing home. In honor of the five witnesses, I crafted a personal and open message, sharing details of my financial mishaps, my parents buying a home for me to rent after I lost a house to foreclosure, and even one cringe-worthy tale of losing electricity due to an unpaid bill.

The room hummed and murmured with kindness, former audience members, coaching clients and even neighborhood friends, smiling and nodding back at me with openhearted reassurance. As I left the front of the room, I was greeted with armfuls of hugs and exclamations of knowing me when. Driving home, the heady buzz made my hands shake as I gripped the steering wheel, overwhelmed with the knowledge every challenge, every heart-constricting moment in my life had a purpose, to uplift the people around me.

Something you should know about flood lights and stages, audiences and podiums, no matter how expansive and light the success feels as you float from the stage, it's nearly impossible to predict the ultimate result of your presentation. Even a standing ovation does not guarantee the satisfaction of the board members or committee or individual who hired you.

And, even though I can close my eyes and experience the waves of life-change I witnessed in that moment during and after "the talk," there was at least one disenchanted person who also had a voice, someone who took the time to type out her observations and feelings. A person who was motivated enough by her own response to my story to fold that piece of paper and after placing it in the envelope to decorate it with stickers in shapes of Shamrocks.

She didn't enjoy my tales of triumph, reminding me not everyone has the safety net of family. Some of us, she wrote, don't live so proudly beyond our means. She didn't like my step-by-step guide to a changed life or the foolhardy belief in fantasies and vision boards. She was sure I had left other audiences deflated and disappointed and recommended I get additional training if I insisted on pursuing this career path. She ended the letter abruptly, without signing her name, wishing me continued "success," the word wrapped in sarcastic quotes.

After I read my first hate mail over and over, leaving makeup-tinged fingerprints on the envelope and letter. After I talked about it to my husband, who kindly reminded me of the sacks filled with plain white envelopes Oprah must receive each month. After I posted about it on Facebook, to receive kind support and challenges to my interpretation of the letter (maybe she was just being constructive- um, no). After it fell on the floor a few times, and I didn't pick it up because I already knew what it would say, I threw it away, only mounting the deceptively cheery envelope with a magnet on my inspiration board.

It would remind me my work is not singularly glorious. To connect beyond the comedic banter and triumphant anecdotes, to plant the seeds of transformation, I must brave the wintery glares and hard hearts of those who will not see my value, who doubt my intention, who prefer another way to change. My first hate mail, will command me to stand in my truth under the lights and click authentically in my five-inch heels on stage, to never sugar coat the lessons and stories. I will find and reach those who need me, even under duress and scorn.

And, I refuse to see my mailbox as anything but a magnificent portal to the outside world, always ready to surprise with something wonder-filled.

Made in the USA
San Bernardino, CA
01 June 2016